Paranormal

STOKE-ON-TRENT

LEOPARD PUB - P/21.

Paranormal
STOKE-ON-TRENT

MATT HICKS AND

TERRI SETTERINGTON

First published 2009

The History Press
The Mill, Brimscombe Port
Stroud, Gloucestershire, GL5 2QG
www.thehistorypress.co.uk

Reprinted 2009, 2010

British Library Cataloguing in Publication Data.
A catalogue record for this book is available from the British Library.

ISBN 978 0 7524 4885 5

Typesetting and origination by The History Press
Printed in Great Britain
Manufacturing managed by Jellyfish Print Solutions Ltd

CONTENTS

ACKNOWLEDGEMENTS

With thanks to: Mel, Nick Duffy at the West Midlands Ghost Club, Martin Jeffrey, Gladstone Pottery Museum, Dave Bradbury, John Easom, and all those who have reported their ghostly experiences!

All images by Nathan Fox unless stated otherwise.

INTRODUCTION

Sitting as it does between the bigger and more famous cities of Manchester and Birmingham, Stoke-on-Trent seems to get overlooked in many respects. Yet Stoke was once the centre of the country's pottery industry and Reginald Mitchell, designer of the Spitfire, hailed from these parts. If the theory is true and many hauntings are closely linked to past events then Stoke should have its fair share of ghosts.

In 2006 I co-founded the Staffordshire Paranormal Study Group, dedicated to unearthing and investigating these hauntings. We take a rational view of such things, and by adopting this approach we tend to uncover as many instances of misinterpretation as what could be termed paranormal. Yet even if we find only one genuinely interesting case in a thousand it is still worthwhile. Over the years I have seen apparitions, had stones thrown at me by an invisible force and heard a variety of frankly very scary disembodied sounds. From the once-glorious houses of Trentham Hall and Alton Towers to eerie occurrences in more modest surroundings, I have found myself sat in the dark (and often the cold) in a variety of places along with my fellow investigators Terri, Sean, Mel, Leanne and Mark.

One thing I've learned is that Stoke has as many strange tales to tell as any other city of its size. If anything, I think the post-industrial malaise that still seems to affect the city makes it a far more curious proposition than more illustrious regenerated centres. Certainly, a lack of national attention and low coverage in popular ghost guides means investigating many of Stoke's haunted locations and stories is a fresher and more involving task than re-hashing material from better- known places.

Both Terri and I were keen for this book not to be a simple recitation of local stories, although for balance, and to show the depth of folklore to be found in these parts, we have included a fair share of myths and legends. Wherever possible, we have attempted to provide any likely rational explanations for the stories, as well as any current thinking, theories or research that we are aware of that may throw some light on what are, in the main, unsolved mysteries. I have had some great first-hand experience of haunted locations, as has Terri who has worked for a number of years at the city's two main hospitals. Her section on the startling variety of strange phenomena that have been reported there over the years makes for fascinating reading.

Many people are sceptical, or even cynical, about the existence of paranormal phenomena and in truth many examples of what at first appear paranormal have a very earthly explanation. Yet despite over a century of what was first termed psychical research and is now known as parapsychology, there still remains a core of accounts that cannot be explained rationally. In addition to the classic reports of ghosts, poltergeists and other hauntings, the Stoke region also boasts what has in recent times been termed a 'window area'. That is to say, a patch that seems to attract the gamut of phenomena, including strange beasts, UFOs and spectral legends.

Ultimately, we both hope this book offers a balanced and informative account of paranormal occurrences in the city of Stoke and the immediate locale. This is a book with the city and history of Stoke-on-Trent at its heart, and the lion's share deals with the city of Stoke and the wider Potteries Urban Area. That said, we have allowed ourselves to stray a little further when we have felt there are tales worth telling. After all, neighbouring places like Alton Towers and Little Moreton Hall, as well as many of the villages and small towns that border Stoke, have as much a part to play in the city's haunted past and present as does any potbank or canal. Hopefully, the book provides new material for research and simply for the pleasure of reading about events that may hint at a world beyond the earthly veil.

Matt Hicks & Terri Setterington, 2009

AN A-Z OF PARANORMAL STOKE-ON-TRENT

ALTON

For its small size, the village of Alton has a great deal of history and a high number of strange and spooky tales. In fact, you could make a good argument for Alton being the most haunted village in North Staffordshire and quite possibly even further afield. The Alton Towers estate has long been the focus of myth and legend and, in recent times, television shows and a record-breaking ghost hunting event have served to heighten its renown. The village of Alton, however, also boasts a castle dating back to the twelfth century, and local legend has it that this too is haunted, although there are no first-hand reports to speak of.

Alton Castle. Dating to the twelfth century, the castle at Alton sits high above the village, which is reputed to be one of the most haunted in the area.

Legend also has it that nearby Slain Hollow was the site of a mighty battle in Saxon times, and it is said that processions of spectral monks are witnessed throughout the area and down to the neighbouring villages. It would be easy to assume that this is just local hearsay, but the story of an unfortunate BT engineer deepens the mystery.

Near to the village of Alton is a telephone exchange building that has gained a reputation amongst engineers for being haunted, to the extent that few will work there alone. Doors are said to slam by themselves and disembodied footsteps heard. Whilst working alone one day, an engineer heard a banging at the windows and looked up to see what reports describe as, 'fifteen to twenty medieval monks with big clubs and furious looks on their faces banging at the windows trying to get in at him'. Managing to run out of the building and start his van, the unfortunate man made his getaway, noticing the monks in his rear view mirror. However, two more monks appeared in front of him and 'started running towards him with furious faces and trying to hit the car with their sticks'. As he passed them he noticed that one of the men was black, which seems strange considering their medieval appearance. It is said that the poor fellow was so shaken by the incident that he was off work for several months afterwards.

Alton Towers. Thought to be an ancient site, and home to many ghost stories. (By kind permission of the James Smith Noel Collection, Louisiana State University in Shreveport)

Alton Towers

Both the house and grounds of Alton Towers had been a place of recreation and pleasure long before the arrival of the rollercoasters. During the late eighteenth and early nineteenth centuries, two successive Earls of Shrewsbury transformed what had been a modest hunting lodge surrounded by plain countryside into a palatial residence with spectacular gardens. During the Victorian era Alton Towers was reputedly the largest private residence in Europe, and the public were periodically welcomed in to wander the glades and grottos. However, disputes within the Shrewsbury family meant that the estate was eventually sold. Today the ruinous Gothic-revival pile is the perfect setting for ghost tours, and most weekends the intrepid and the brave can be found searching for spirits throughout the Towers' dark corridors.

One of the most famous legends connected with the Towers is that of the chained oak, popularised thanks to the Hex ride which is now located in part of the old house. The story goes that when out riding on his Alton estate one day, the Earl of Shrewsbury was met by a gypsy beggar. The earl turned him away in no uncertain terms, leading the aggrieved gypsy to point at a nearby oak and swear that every time a branch fell the Shrewsbury heir apparent would die. This seemed to scare the family enough to have every limb of the cursed tree chained up to prevent them from falling. This version of the tale is just the latest in a number of interpretations, but the oak is real enough and is still bound by iron chains, although a storm in 2007 left it severely damaged. As with all legends of this sort the origins are blurred by time, but it is true that the Shrewsburys have struggled to provide male heirs, with the title often passing to a cousin or another more distant relative.

A good place to start a look around the Towers is the former grand entrance, which is now the queuing system for Hex. Originally, this would have been a very impressive affair; flanked by two stone Talbot dogs, visitors would have ascended the stairs, passing through the great wooden doors into the armoury. Wandering past numerous reminders of the Shrewsburys' long and distinguished history, the path led through the picture gallery and the conservatory before arriving at the house proper. In total, a modest entrance hall of more than 400ft! Despite being a somewhat liminal part of the house, it seems this area is one of the most haunted. It is thought that a coach house stood here previously, but there are few historical clues as to the strange activity. For many years in the twentieth century, the armoury and picture gallery were the main gift shop, and many staff remember experiencing unexplained feelings of intimidation and discomfort. Stranger still, those opening the shop in the morning would sometimes be confronted by items, carefully stacked in pyramids on the floor, despite the area being tidy the previous evening.

Thrill-seekers queuing for Hex have sometimes reported glimpsing a black presence as they file through, and it has been suggested that this apparition is dressed in riding gear. If so, it may be linked to stories of a phantom horseman that is said to ride throughout the estate. Although the activity seems real enough, we can only speculate on the cause. Some say it is one of the former earls; Charles, the 15th, or John the 16th are the most likely candidates since it was they who oversaw the majority of the building work.

In the family tradition, both Charles and John were devout Catholics and the chapel was a central part of life at the Towers. Even in its current state it is quite impressive, especially as the roof has been carefully restored to how it would have appeared after renovation by the architect A.W.N. Pugin. Sitting outside the chapel one evening waiting to take a tour, I and several others heard the distinct sound of a choir singing, despite the place being empty. After speaking to staff, I found that this was a common experience. The chapel was the site of grand and important services, including the funeral of the 16th Earl, and if hauntings are indeed a product of memorable and emotional past events, then it seems logical for the chapel to have its fair share.

Curiously, one of the most frequently witnessed ghosts is not a member of the Talbot family and seems to enjoy roaming the kitchen and servant areas. She has come to be known as the Black Lady, as reports detail a female presence – possibly dressed in dark Victorian clothes – who brings with her an uneasy feeling and the smell of lavender. A common area to meet her is said to be the erstwhile servants' rooms in the basement, although she is said to also wander the upper floor. Popular myth claims that in life she lost a child, and so wears black in mourning.

Theme park visitors are welcome to walk around the ruins during the day, and a number of reports have come from people who decided to take a wander and got a little more than they bargained for! Researcher Martin Jeffrey has gathered witness testimonies from Alton Towers for several years now, including this curious incident that occurred a few summers ago:

I received a report from a young lady called Sally Preston, who witnessed the ghost of a tall gentleman in the library area. Sally had an interest in the paranormal and especially ghosts; she had heard that the ruins were haunted and so she ventured in with her dad. They walked for over twenty minutes when they realised that they could hear music coming from downstairs and seemingly from the library. As they stood quiet there was a sudden rush of footsteps and a shadowy figure passed outside in the corridor towards the banqueting hall. Intrigued, Sally undertook some research and found that she recognised the ghost as the 20th Earl of Shrewsbury, Charles Talbot, the man who had sold Alton Towers after financial difficulties in the 1920s. He is described as tall, with a crooked nose and a thin moustache and wearing full military uniform. It is said that if you stand in front of the shadow, it will bump into you, knocking you to the ground.

It is interesting that this account refers to paranormal activity moving towards the banqueting hall, as over the years a range of reports have come from this area. People often feel intimidated and unwelcome; perhaps this is down to the presence of the truculent earl that Sally Preston seemed to encounter?

Physical paranormal activity is regularly experienced, especially near to the doors leading across to the other entertaining rooms. In 2008 a friend of mine was leading a vigil in the banqueting hall, and asked for a bump or bang. The doors were obligingly banged shut. Wanting to verify whether the cause was natural, he asked twice more and both times was promptly rewarded with the same sound. Upon request, the door then swung open. Again on request, the group were then greeted with several guttural groans – a rather scary encounter, and one that seems very unlikely to have happened by sheer chance.

Some would argue that inherently spooky places like Alton Towers will always lead people to assume a paranormal explanation for things that are in fact perfectly rational. However, having had regular personal experience of the place and bearing in mind the range of bizarre first-hand reports, I don't believe that we should settle for such a simplistic explanation.

BIDDULPH

Located just north of the city, Biddulph sits on the edge of the Moorlands area. An Iron-Age hillfort and the remains of an ancient burial cairn – known as the Bridestones – are located here. The Bridestones were once a considerable local landmark, thought to stretch some 100m in length, but they were, for want of a better word, vandalised by eighteenth-century road builders eager to find a cheap source of stone. It is sad that this once imposing monument, which some suggest to be unique in this country, is now in a poor state of disrepair.

Given its long history and evidently important role to pre-Christian religion, we should not be surprised that Biddulph and the immediate area hold a number of strange tales. It is said that a tributary of the River Dane that runs close to Halls Road in the town was once known as 'Ghost River' and that the ghost of a woman wearing pale clothing (reports differ as to whether these are grey or white) haunts the banks.

Knypersley

Knypersley Reservoir lies south of the town. It is an eerie place at the best of times and has long been considered a place of power by those interested in mysticism. Local author Doug Pickford records that renowned antiquarian, mystic and Staffordshire native Elias Ashmole – he who gave his name to Oxford's famous Ashmolean Museum – visited Knypersley Reservoir on at least one occasion.

The Bridestones was once a much more imposing place of ancient ritual. (T. Setterington)

In the woods above the water are found the Gawton Stone and Gawton's Well, both of which are said to have healing properties. The name Gawton is believed to come from a hermit of that name who was cured by their power and continued to live nearby. The well is thought to be the location of a holy place or sacred grove used by the Druids of Celtic culture, although it is unclear as to whether the magical reputation of the area is thanks to these rumours or vice versa. Certainly, wells, springs and other water sources occupy an important place in folklore. Pre-Christian belief was that a spirit protected the sources of water and that worshipping these beings would bring a cure for illnesses. When the Christians arrived, the practice of visiting these holy wells continued, although the resident spirits were exchanged for saints. The name Knypersley is understood to have its origins in old words for 'oak' and 'knowledge' and the well itself is surrounded by a number of yew trees, which themselves occupy an important place in ancient Celtic culture.

Biddulph Grange and Gardens

Pickford also brings our attention to the fact that land in the Knypersley area was later owned by one James Bateman, proprietor of the nearby Biddulph Grange.

Knypersley Reservoir. The name Knypersley is understood to have its origins in old words for 'oak' and 'knowledge', suggesting ancient ritual use.

The Gawton Stone. Legend has it that the Gawton Stone holds mystical healing powers.

Gawton's Well. The well lies within a grove of yew trees and is said to have been in use as far back as the time of the druids.

There is the suggestion that Bateman may have known and involved himself with the mystical reputation of the Gawton Stone and Gawton's Well; whether this is true or not, Biddulph Grange is certainly home to a number of strange stories and rumours.

It is thought that the site of the grange has been inhabited since at least Saxon times. In the sixteenth century records state that much of the contemporary house was destroyed during the Civil War by the notorious 'Roaring Meg' cannon. By the time Bateman moved to the house in 1840 it was described as just a 'simple rectory'. Rich from interests in various local industries, Bateman greatly extended the building, transforming it into a grand hall and spent further time and money on the elaborate gardens, but by 1861 the family sold up and moved to London. After a fire had destroyed much of the property in 1896, it was partially rebuilt and later became a hospital.

Today, most of the building is taken up with private apartments and the rest is occupied by the National Trust, which also cares for the gardens. Many believe that Bateman's greatest legacy is not the house but the gardens, which wind down from the patio into areas separated to showcase plants and styles from around the globe. Bateman and his father were both noted botanists, and the garden was begun at a time when the British Empire was at its height. It seems the garden design was intended to show off exotic plants that had been brought back from all corners of the globe, which in turn would speak volumes about Bateman's power, knowledge and wealth.

The garden contains a number of mythical and mystical elements, not least an Egyptian section with a statue depicting the deity Thoth in ape form. Given that Bateman is reputed to have been a Freemason, this choice of Egyptian deity is an interesting one. Regularly depicted in humanoid form with the head of an ibis or an ape, Thoth was thought by the ancient Egyptians to have once reigned on Earth for some 3,000 years and he was worshipped by them as the originator of both human and divine knowledge. The Greeks considered Thoth to be the selfsame god as their own Hermes, and through this both deities have come to be known as Hermes Trismegistus. A hermetic tradition supposedly based on the teachings of Hermes appeared in the Middle Ages, influencing both Freemasonic rituals and occultists such as Aleister Crowley, who wrote *The Book of Thoth*. Freemasons consider Thoth to have been vital in preserving and continuing much knowledge crucial to their practices, and as such he is seen as an important figure.

With this in mind, we should perhaps consider why James Bateman had chosen to put a statue of Thoth in his garden. Of course, we need to bear in mind that the Victorians were prone to co-opting appealing fragments of different cultures, as is the case with much of the garden at Biddulph Grange. However, the strong occult and esoteric connections to Thoth, combined with Bateman's alleged Freemasonic leanings, mean we need to be open to the possibility that this part of the garden was intended to have some higher purpose than aesthetic appeal.

BIDDULPH GRANGE

Biddulph Grange, home of the magical gardens developed by James Bateman.
(T. Setterington)

Furthermore, the Egyptian temple at Biddulph has a crucial role to play in the plot of *The Green Stone*, a book by Graham Phillips and Martin Keatman that popularised the activity of psychic questing, where strange phenomena are apparently harnessed to unravel esoteric mysteries. The book and its sequel, *The Eye of Fire*, have their roots in the mythology of the philosopher's stone which, perhaps not entirely coincidentally, is thought to have been the emerald tablet owned by Hermes Trismegistus. In the late 1970s Phillips, Keatman and a number of friends began to receive apparently psychic messages and experiences that all linked to a green stone called 'Meonia'. One of these people was a psychic based in Alsager who claimed to keep hearing the name Meonia in his mind but had no idea what it could mean. He later discovered that Graham Phillips and his friend Andrew Collins had similar experiences entirely independently. This led to a detailed and labyrinthine mystery, involving a number of locations close to Stoke and a man called Terry Shotton who at the time lived in the Blythe Bridge area of the city. *The Eye of Fire* followed several years later and detailed the search for a red companion to the green stone. The book contained a greater role for Shotton and included local landmarks such as Dovedale and Ranton Abbey near Stafford.

The link to Biddulph Grange begins some way into *The Green Stone*, when four of the group are meditating to try and seek greater details of the increasingly complex mystery. Graham Phillips receives the distinct image of an Egyptian temple somewhere in the Midlands, feels it has been used by a secret society and that the name Mary Heath was somehow important. However, it is not until Terry Shotton has spoken to a friend based in Stoke that the group realise the image may be that of Biddulph Grange. Upon visiting the temple, the group link it to a mysterious Victorian society called The Nine and find out that former owners of the Grange were Robert Heath and his wife Mary. These clues lead the group to try and contact Mary Heath through a séance, and gain important further suggestions as to where the quest may lead.

Some people are sceptical about the truth behind both *The Green Stone* and *The Eye of Fire*. Certainly, the second book took a more sensational line than the first and it can sometimes be hard to believe that such remarkable things could happen at all, let alone so frequently. However, what is interesting is that despite a considerable number of people being involved in some way through the course of the two books, there has been no public denial or exposé over the interceding twenty years and more. Unfortunately Terry Shotton died recently and so the chance to ask him about his opinion on the matter has passed. Nevertheless, he was a respected member of national UFO group BUFORA and several people who knew him felt he regarded the events of both books to be genuine. Whatever your view, the whole affair remains a mystery, with North Staffordshire playing a crucial part.

BURSLEM

Known as the 'Mother Town' of the Potteries, Burslem is recorded in the Domesday Book as a small farming settlement. The pottery industry for which it is famous began here in early times; it is thought that the good quality of local clay meant pots were being made in the area from the late twelfth century onwards. Much improved transport links in the eighteenth century allowed rapid expansion into a typical industrial centre, with a range of important potbanks situated round and about. The town has some of the finest architecture in the city, and some say that there is more industrial heritage to be found along the Burslem stretch of the Trent and Mersey Canal than anywhere else in the country. It is perhaps most famous nationally for the author Arnold Bennett who used many of the local landmarks in his books, often with thinly disguised names such as Bursley.

The Leopard Hotel

The Leopard has been in use as a pub since at least 1765, ideally placed in the town centre to make the most of the growing population. Ambitious local brewer James Norris purchased the building in 1872 and expanded it to a large fifty-seven bedroom hotel. Norris' brewery was situated just across the street, and it is thought that the tunnels still to be seen in the cellar were made at this

The Leopard Hotel. The building has a rich history and is said to be haunted by a number of ghosts.

time to provide a convenient passage between the sites of beer production and sale. It has been speculated that the building was not always the most upmarket of public houses and at times played host to rather unsavoury characters, with some rooms used by prostitutes. Perhaps due to its large size, the Leopard could not sustain the trade needed to maintain itself and by the 1950s many of the rooms had been boarded up. Although the front areas of the building were kept in good condition and still used as a pub, the rear bedrooms remained out of bounds until new owners bought the property several years ago. Letting curiosity get the better of them they opened up the dusty old passages and discovered what amounted to a time capsule, with original fixtures and fittings still in place throughout.

The Leopard is certainly an atmospheric place to seek paranormal experiences, and is very popular with local ghost hunting groups. Although this can often make the job of sifting through for genuinely interesting reports difficult, the Leopard's current owners and staff seem genuine about a number of strange experiences they have witnessed themselves. The function rooms to the rear of the ground floor are said to be haunted, with noises as if tables are being cleared or set often heard despite there being no staff in the area. It is claimed that a number of upper rooms have a dark and depressing feel to them, linked to prostitution and even murder. In what seems to be typical activity for haunted pubs, glasses are said to move and fall off shelves on their own. More extreme claims of paranormal activity there include people being pushed and even being grabbed by the throat.

Molly Leigh

Of late, some people have been linking the Leopard with the story of Molly Leigh, another local legend, but there is little evidence in older accounts to suggest any connection between the two. Nevertheless, the tale of Molly Leigh is one of few local legends to gain wider recognition. This is largely down to Sybil Leek, known as 'Britain's most famous witch' in the 1950s, whose family came from Stoke-on-Trent and claimed to be descended from Molly. Although there is some doubt over whether Leek's claims are accurate, what is certain is that those who openly practiced witchcraft have suffered persecution for centuries, and, along with the more recent plight of Helen Duncan, the story of Molly Leigh has become something of a symbol for that suffering.

Molly's full name was Margaret Leigh. She was born around the year 1685 in Burslem, which at that point was little more than a small country town neighbouring the Moorlands. It's claimed that Molly was something of an oddity from birth — choosing to suckle from animals and chewing on stale bread even before her teeth had developed. She was not helped by her famed bad looks and the early death of her parents, which forced her into a lonely existence on the outskirts of town, keeping cows. She was a regular sight around Burslem as she delivered milk, her pet blackbird perched on her shoulder. Even before the rumours of witchcraft began Molly was subject to accusations of selling bad milk.

It is unclear precisely how or why the rumours did begin, but local people began to claim that the blackbird was a sign of witchcraft. The local Revd Spencer did little to abate the situation by publicly claiming that Molly rarely attended church – in those days a serious social *faux pas*. The story goes that, angered by the reverend's claims, Molly sent her blackbird to spy on him at his favourite drinking haunt, the Turk's Head. It's alleged that when the bird appeared atop the pub sign the beer turned sour and the customers suddenly developed rheumatism. The reverend fetched his gun and took a shot at the bird, but missed, after which he was bedridden for days with mysterious stomach pains.

Molly's unpopularity grew and grew, until the people of Burslem began to blame her for anything unexplained or unfortunate that happened to them. She became increasingly unwelcome in town, and is thought to have lived out the rest of her days in solitude aside from her pet blackbird. It was said that the bush outside her cottage, a favourite perch of the blackbird, never blossomed. She died in 1748.

Molly's death was just the beginning of the myth. Legend has it that shortly after her burial a group led by Revd Spencer went to Molly's cottage in search of the malevolent blackbird. Looking through the grimy windows, they found no bird. Instead they were shocked to see Molly herself sitting peacefully by the fire in her rocking chair mumbling to herself, 'Weight and measure sold I never. Milk and water sold I never.'

Rumours of witchcraft were reignited and spread throughout the town. Had the folk of Burslem really lived all these years with a powerful witch amongst them? What would be the revenge for her ill treatment? Matters were not helped when the blackbird became a regular sight once more, pecking and harassing people and crowing into the small hours.

The good men and women of Burslem soon had all they could take of the troublesome bird and it was Revd Spencer once again who decided to take action, summoning together a group of local priests to deal with Molly once and for all. One midnight in April, they travelled to the graveyard at St John's with a mysterious sack. They set to the earth with shovels – it must have been an oddly amusing sight to see a group of be-cassocked priests toiling away like farmhands. However, holy men or no, they succeeded at the grim task of exhuming Molly's body and drove a stake through her heart. The blackbird was grabbed from the sack and bundled, still alive, into the coffin. In a final attempt to do away with Molly, they repositioned the casket on a distinctly un-Christian north–south alignment, and swiftly resealed the lid.

It appears that the actions of the reverend and his gang of cassock-cronies worked. There are various subsequent reports of Molly roaming Burslem, and black shades seen in the graveyard, but most versions of the story have it that her influence over the folk of Burslem ends with her reburial. It is natural that over time, and especially given the amount of pubs in the town, a number of different versions of such a popular tale will crop up. Furthermore, there are claims that the grave found in St John's churchyard may actually be medieval or earlier, which leads us to question whether the final stage of the story is a later addition used to neatly explain the existence of a strange old grave in the churchyard whilst adding extra drama to Molly's story.

The intriguing thing is that the legend, in any form, has endured for so long. There are no other local folk tales that seem to capture the imagination quite like Molly's. Its legacy is visible today through Halloween dares and even a play about her life. Whether witch or victim, Molly Leigh's story has become one of the most told in the area, and her alleged grave has become a popular attraction for folklorists and dares alike. It's said that she will appear to anyone brave enough to run round her grave and recite the lines, 'Molly Leigh, Molly Leigh, can't catch me' three times.

Ford Green Hall

The village of Smallthorne sits a little way out of Burslem and is home to one of the most distinctive historic buildings in the city. Built as a farmhouse in the early seventeenth century and extended several times over the years, Ford Green Hall once stood in over thirty acres of farmland. It was home to the Ford family, who were influential yeoman farmers and lived here for around 200 years. It is now a popular museum used regularly for school visits.

Perhaps because it is the only building of its type in the city, Ford Green Hall attracts plenty of speculation as to its possible hauntings. Although evidence suggesting ghostly activity is scarce and the house has a warm and welcoming feel, there is one notable feature – walk into the middle room downstairs and you will notice a series of strange symbols above the fireplace. Their origin and purpose are unknown, as the panelling was found in the loft whilst the building was being restored. I have consulted a number of occult specialists on the symbols and the general consensus is that these were intended as some form of magical protection from malign forces. As the hall was built during a time when many people were highly aware of alleged dangers from witchcraft and magic, a likely explanation is that they are intended to prevent witches and bad luck from entering the house. Perhaps the most striking of the symbols is an upturned pentagram; although to many people this may suggest Satanism and other dark practices, historically the symbol has much wider and far less sinister meanings. Furthermore, there is the possibility that some or all of the symbols were reinstalled upside down, which would mean the pentagram was originally a more conventional upright example.

Beyond them being used for protection, there seems to be no definite answer as to precisely what the symbols may mean. It would have been common practice in past centuries to visit local wise or 'cunning' folk in order to seek advice on how to protect yourself and your property from witches and bad magic. The type and form of advice and counter-magic used varies greatly throughout the UK, with common magical texts often integrated and interpreted into a vernacular or even personal style. This seems to be the case at Ford Green Hall, where the symbols bear a strong resemblance to those found in contemporary texts and interpretations of these practiced by cunning folk in other areas of the country.

CAVERSWALL

It is thought that the history of Caverswall and its castle stretches as far back as Saxon times, and possibly even earlier. The manor of 'Cavreswalle' is found in the Domesday Book and it is known that in 1275 a knight of King Edward II, Sir William de Caverswall, was permitted to fortify the site of the current castle.

When the Black Death reached Caverswall in 1349 the villagers blamed a local witch called Agnes, who was burned at the stake as a result. This was not the only time that the vengeful locals pointed the finger of blame. In 1783 the Laki volcanic fault in Iceland erupted and emitted huge amounts of sulphur dioxide into the skies over Europe. Thought to be three times the amount of sulphur dioxide produced by European industry throughout the whole of 2006, the resulting fog was so bad that many ships were forced to stay in port and thousands lost their lives. It is also said to have turned the moon a blood-red colour, which the villagers of Caverswall blamed on the supernatural powers of one Lady Vane, the recently deceased mistress of their master at Caverswall Castle.

More recently, there have been reports of a ghostly child in a white nightdress around the area of the road to Blythe Bridge. There have also been sightings around here of what is described as an 'orange-coloured shape' floating above the footpath.

CUNNING FOLK AND FAMOUS WITCHES

In times gone by, many people relied on the skills of local wise and cunning folk in much the same way we do with doctors today. Such practices have only begun to fade surprisingly recently, and today there are still people throughout the country who practice the old ways. A respectable living could be made from mystical skills, and, although there are published examples of fraud and deception, the enduring appeal of cunning folk suggests that many were believed to have genuine magic abilities. Stoke-on-Trent would have been no different to any other area of the country, especially given its rural setting prior to the industrial revolution. Alongside Molly Leigh, the towns hereabout would have been home to a variety of people practising magic and the like down the years. Below are two examples that have passed into local legend.

Caverswall stocks. When the Black Death reached Caverswall in 1349 the villagers blamed a local witch called Agnes, who was burned at the stake as a result.

Sybil Leek

The most famous local witch, at least of the last century, was Sybil Leek. Born in Normacot, she came from a long line of witches that claimed lineage back to Molly Leigh herself. As you might expect of a family that counted Aleister Crowley as a firm friend, Sybil was immersed in esoteric matters from a young age and for a time in the twentieth century she was one of the most renowned astrologers in the world. It seems she had her grandmother to thank for these skills, as she is said to have given readings for a host of famous names such as

Thomas Hardy and Lawrence of Arabia. Yet Sybil's life was not entirely devoted to witchcraft; before finding fame she ran a chain of antique shops in and around the New Forest. However, by the 1950s she had decided to be open about her beliefs and practices with the aim to educate and change opinion at a time when such things were looked on less favourably than they are today. This brought her increasing media attention which eventually began to make her unpopular with some of the people in the village where she lived. When negative local opinion forced her to leave, she moved to the United States and began to appear on television and radio shows with parapsychologist Hans Holzer. She died in Florida in 1982.

According to some, Leek also used her apparent supernatural powers to good effect during the Second World War. She was asked to create fake astrological readings for members of the Nazi party, such as Rudolf Hess, who held a belief in such things. Despite being something of a role model for many modern witches, Leek's views on witchcraft were often highly conservative. She is known to have disapproved of nudity and drug taking during rituals, yet held a strong belief in more traditional practices such as cursing.

Sybil Leek is a popular figure to this day, primarily because of her bravery to stand up for her religious beliefs despite the evident difficulties it brought her. We must remember that as recently as the 1940s medium Helen Duncan had been tried and imprisoned under the Witchcraft Act, which was only repealed in 1951. For many, practicing witchcraft was a rather clandestine and very private activity, yet Leek was open about her beliefs and intent on providing a positive example of what it meant to be a witch.

Ma and Pa Hatton

The plight of Molly Leigh, detailed in the Burslem section, is not the only example of local prejudice against apparently innocent people; in the seventeenth century the ire of folk in Bagnall was focussed on an elderly couple by the name of Hatton. The suspicion that the Hattons possessed magical powers seems to stem from the fact that Pa Hatton delighted in running through the local woods at night making strange animal noises, and that Ma Hatton had a curious squint in one of her eyes. These events are said to have occurred at a time when fear of witchcraft was at a peak with self-proclaimed Witchfinder General Matthew Hopkins stoking fear and a sense of paranoia against those with unusual features or behaviour.

One such feature would have been a strangely coloured, lazy or squinting eye, which could be regarded as an 'evil eye'. It is thought belief in the evil eye dates back millennia, and most likely started in the Eastern Mediterranean region. It spread across Asia and up into northern Europe as travel and trade between the regions increased. Whilst several formal descriptions of the evil eye state that the possessor does not necessarily have to be malicious, or even aware that they are causing harm, at least here in England it came to be used in connection with witches and wilful misdoings.

Possession of an alleged evil eye may well have condemned many innocent women. Certainly, in the rather paranoid atmosphere of the seventeenth century Ma Hatton's squint would have been enough to mark her out as having strange powers. However, the Hattons might have been left alone in their remote cottage if it wasn't for the fact that Pa Hatton's activities meant the villagers had to restrain him and deliver him home.

Predictably, a range of unfortunate ailments and ills that befell the villagers and their livestock were blamed on the Hattons and their weird ways. A popular story told to illustrate this concerns one Joseph Cope, who discovered one day that his cow refused to give milk. Cope leapt to the conclusion that Ma Hatton had a grudge against him and had cursed his poor cow to teach him a lesson. He gathered a few burly friends and marched up to the Hatton's cottage to force the curse to be lifted.

Yet Ma Hatton was understandably reluctant to oblige. Resorting to violence, Cope is said to have threatened her with an axe until she relented and blessed the poor cow. I don't suppose we will ever know whether Ma Hatton was really a witch, but folklore has it that the cow soon recovered, only deepening the suspicion of the villagers.

HANCHURCH

Hanchurch is little more than a hamlet lying almost uncomfortably close to the M6 outside Newcastle-under-Lyme. In *A Guide to Staffordshire and the Black Country*, Michael Raven talks of a local legend that claims there was a church here, but that it was moved to Trentham by four white creatures, variously said to be mice, swans or oxen. Given the fact that Trentham Church dates to at least Anglo-Saxon times it seems possible that the holy site here at Hanchurch was superseded by the coming of Christians to Trentham. Perhaps the myth outlined by Michael Raven is a folk memory of this event passed down through storytelling.

The woods surrounding Hanchurch are notorious for being haunted, and rumour has it that witch covens and other occultists hold ceremonies in these parts. One story, quite possibly an urban myth of sorts, tells of how a young couple entered the woods with amorous intentions but soon came out solemn faced, refusing to speak about what they saw.

My partner used to travel to work along a road that skirts Hanchurch woods and about six o'clock one morning saw several very bright lights flash on and off in the woods very quickly. She says that, despite travelling the road for the best part of six months at that time of the morning, she never saw anything like it again.

The lights were too bright to be a flashlight and seemed to be pointing to the sky. Interestingly, this was at a time in early 2006 when a number of UFO reports were coming from the same area.

HANLEY

Even before the creation of the city in 1910, Hanley was often described as the 'capital of the Potteries'. In terms of industry, Hanley and neighbouring areas such as Shelton and Etruria are fairly typical, with potbanks, coal mines and iron foundries scattered around. The town is now home to the city's principal shopping centre and also Festival Park.

The Etruria White Rabbit

Built by potter Josiah Wedgwood and an early example of a factory village in the vein of Port Sunlight or Bourneville, Etruria was at one time separate from its larger neighbour Hanley, with a stretch of wooded countryside between the two. It is known that a murder was committed in this area in the year 1833. Young John Holdcroft was killed by Charles Shaw, who is said to have shown little remorse for his crime even when he was caught and duly deported. This would have been big news locally and sometime after the trial murmurs began about the wooded area being haunted. Folk talked of the eerie sound of a boy crying for help, then the sight of a white rabbit running across the path of whoever had been brave enough to face the woods alone. There is an account of the supposed beast in Henry Wedgwood's *The Romance of Staffordshire*, which describes a 'beautiful milk-white rabbit'. Apparently, so solid was the belief in the existence of the rabbit that one brave man resolved to get to the bottom of the problem and catch it. However, despite seeing the rabbit and being certain he had caught it as he made a desperate lunge, he was rewarded with nothing more than an injured shoulder.

The Potteries Museum and Art Gallery

Sited in Hanley is the Potteries Museum and Art Gallery, the principal museum in the area built in 1956 on the site of Ridgway Pottery's Bell Works. This had been a large potbank, and the company had a royal warrant from Queen Victoria. The museum contains a variety of exhibits on social and natural history, archaeology, and a world-class collection of ceramics. Since 1969 it has also been home to a Mark XVI Supermarine Spitfire, whose designer, Reginald Mitchell, was born and raised locally.

Staff have reported unexplained feelings of unease and a sense of being watched throughout the building, with the Spitfire gallery identified as an area where activity

Hanchurch yews. These trees are thought to date back over 1,000 years.

The view towards Hanchurch woods. The land around Hanchurch, including the woods, has a strong reputation for eerie goings-on.

The Potteries Museum, Hanley. The museum is built on the site of an old pot bank, and has been investigated by paranormal groups on a number of occasions. (By kind permission of the Potteries Museum and Art Gallery)

The Spitfire at the Potteries Museum. People have reported seeing the apparition of a pilot in the cockpit of the plane. (By kind permission of the Potteries Museum and Art Gallery)

seems particularly focussed. Some people have claimed to have seen the apparition of a pilot in the cockpit of the plane, and there are also reports that staff arriving to open up in the mornings often find the canopy open, despite it being closed last thing the night before. Some people believe that the reason behind hauntings in current or former potbanks could be down to the way in which firing pots (or indeed any process involving fire and burning) can alter the magnetic properties of ion particles in some substances, such as soil. This has then been linked into the 'stone tape theory', which suggests that the magnetic properties of stone and other building materials can act as a sort of recording device for emotionally charged experiences which are then somehow 'played back', causing what we see as ghosts, apparitions and the like. It should be pointed out that this has hardly been proven, but it is a theory that has provoked a lot of debate all the same. There is also a suggestion that objects can act in a similar way as the 'stone tape theory' and so the exhibits in museums could be responsible for bringing with them paranormal activity. In the case of the museum's Spitfire this would be disappointing to some extent, as although it travelled with the RAF across Europe it has never seen active service.

The Regent Theatre

No ghost walk of a city centre is complete without a haunted theatre, and Hanley has just the candidate. The subject of a multi-million-pound renovation programme, the Regent Theatre on Piccadilly was reopened in 1999. Although the distinctive modern extension dominates the view of the city from the A500, the main entrance to the Regent is unassuming from street level, and it is necessary to cross the street and look up to see the attractive Art Deco façade. Finished in 1929, the building was commissioned by the Provincial Cinematograph Theatres Co. and was intended to be a prestigious alternative to the cinemas of Manchester and Birmingham. Much of the internal décor survives and gives some strong clues as to the grand appearance originally intended.

Taken over by the Gaumont British Picture Corporation in 1930, The Regent was an important focus for the local community, especially during the war years, and hosted live shows and concerts as well as the first 'talkie' films the city had seen. However, the theatre fell on hard times in the 1970s and despite a name change to the Odeon it finally closed its doors in 1989, remaining empty until its renovation in the late 1990s.

In a similar way to pubs, theatres are almost expected to be haunted and as a result seem to acquire some quite typical ghostly tales. With this in mind, it was refreshing when the Staffordshire Paranormal Study Group paid a visit to the Regent and found that there were few spectres of old actors to be found. Instead, there were strange smells, cold spots and a strong sense of presence in certain areas as well as first-hand reports of the apparition of a young girl who appears from time to time between certain rows of seats.

The stage and orchestra pit are understood to be areas of focus for paranormal activity. We had been told prior to an investigation of the building that other groups had heard a loud and very distinctive banging sound on the stage whilst sitting in the orchestra pit beneath. We were all surprised to hear the selfsame noise later in the night – a loud bang followed by what sounded like a bouncing sound. The few of us present in the building that evening had all been accounted for and a detailed inspection of the area revealed no likely objects that could have caused the sound. Although there could be a rational explanation to be found in the hydraulic machinery that moves the stage, this seems unlikely given that the sound came from the stage floor itself and not from the area beneath.

The Victoria Hall

Along with the Regent Theatre, the Victoria Hall is the other main venue for concerts and shows in Hanley and has also been renovated and modernised in recent times. Renowned for its fine acoustics, 'the Vic' was built in 1888 and is Grade II listed. The neighbouring Town Hall was initially built as the Queen's Hotel and designed to provide high-class accommodation for visitors to Hanley,

Regent Theatre, Hanley. The apparition of a young girl is said to appear in a certain row of seats at this old theatre. (By kind permission of the Ambassador Theatre Group)

Victoria Hall, Hanley. Neighbouring the town hall, the old police cells are now used as changing rooms for performers. (By kind permission of the Ambassador Theatre Group)

The Place nightclub, Hanley. The spirit of a young woman is said to haunt the top floor.

this never really proved profitable and in 1888 the building was acquired for the city. For some years the local police station was situated within the Town Hall and at some stage rooms to the rear were extended and converted for use as prison cells. These rooms now belong to the Victoria Hall and are used as dressing rooms. Visiting performers often remark on an unwelcome and heavy feeling in this area. Although the rooms are rather strangely shaped, it is not obvious that they were once cells and it seems unlikely that people are putting two and two together to assume these are former cells haunted by previous occupants. Strangely, staff often have trouble operating electrical equipment in this area and this is sometimes connected to ghostly activity. Furthermore, a number of people have reported hearing strange sounds around the stage and auditorium.

The Place

Across the other side of the city centre is a nightclub known for many years as 'The Place'. A highly popular destination for revellers in the 1960s, the building has long had a reputation for being haunted, with the majority of stories focussing on the apparition of a woman. One report describes how a member of staff approached a woman who was crying on the top floor of the venue to see what was wrong, but the woman promptly walked away and exited through a door marked 'staff only'. The employee followed the woman closely, but on the other side of the door she was nowhere to be seen.

Captain Edward John Smith and the Titanic

Born in Hanley on the 27 January 1850 at 51 Well Street, Edward John Smith was an only child. Following an education at Etruria Middle School he started his seafaring career at the age of thirteen. With much experience under his belt, Edward Smith joined the White Star Line in March 1880, receiving his first White Star command on the SS *Republic* in 1887. Rapid promotion followed and in 1903 he was honoured by King Edward VII for his war service and awarded the Transport Medal, favouring Smith as a 'safe captain'. He seemed a natural choice when he was appointed in command of the RMS *Titanic*, the greatest and largest steamship of all time, which left Southampton docks for her maiden voyage on 10 April 1912. Her short, sad and familiar story ends on 14 April 1912, when at 11.40 p.m. she struck an iceberg in the North Atlantic, 700 kilometres from the coast of Newfoundland. The ship took two hours and forty minutes to sink and in that time nearly 1,500 passengers and crew had lost their lives. It proved to be one of the biggest maritime accidents in the history of sea travel.

Much myth and mystery surrounds the loss of the *Titanic*. The huge boat was never christened and a cockerel is said to have crowed as the boat pulled out of the harbour – both events are regarded as bad omens by sailors. Seventeen workers are known to have died during construction of the *Titanic*, two of which are believed to haunt the Harland & Wolff's Belfast shipyard to this day. Amid the fury of religious contention in Ireland, Protestant workers were accused of attempting to sabotage the ship, with the *Titanic's* hull number 3909-04 offered as evidence. Catholic workers reported that if the numbers were viewed backwards they read 'NO-POPE'.

It is also believed that the *Titanic* was transporting Egyptian artefacts and a mummy of an unidentified pharaoh in its hold, which were on their way to a museum in America. The mummy was already regarded as accursed and had been nicknamed as such by the press of the day. It is believed that everyone who had even photographed the mummy had met an untimely death and even during its time on the dockside it was instrumental in breaking a dockworker's leg when the casket in which it laid was unceremoniously dropped during transportation. Did the curse of the mummy play a hand in the sinking of the *Titanic*?

HAUNTED ROADS

The M6

In 2006, the *Guardian* reported that a survey, to collect accounts of spooky activity on roads throughout the UK, had concluded that the M6 was the most haunted road in the country. According to the survey, stories from the M6 ranged from Roman soldiers along the toll road section, to a phantom truck seen by writer and researcher Paul Devereux.

The stretch of the M6 that runs past Stoke is certainly not blessed with good luck – traffic jams and accidents are frequent, and recently there have been a spate of terrible fatalities. Folklore has come to explain this accident blackspot by pinning responsibility on a band of Scottish soldiers that was retreating from the Battle of Worcester during the English Civil War. Legend has it that they set up camp one night in an area that the M6 now passes through, but were massacred by locals from nearby Sandbach. Apparently many drivers on the motorway are distracted by ghostly figures flitting across the highway. In a rather stereotypical twist, it is said that one of the most regularly seen ghosts is that of a bagpiper.

Considering this story's links to the Civil War, it is well worth noting an experience at Keele motorway services in the 1970s. Two football fans returning from an away game saw a man dressed in Puritan clothes exiting the toilets, yet when they decided to follow him he was nowhere to be found. Further enquiries with other visitors and staff drew a blank. Often persecuted in England for their belief, when Cromwell won the Civil War the Puritans enjoyed a brief period of respite until the restoration of the monarchy in 1660. Perhaps this is simply a coincidence, but it seems strange that these two stories should both focus on one small area of the M6.

A number of roads in the area have a haunted reputation, including this one between Trentham and Longton.

The A5035 Longton-Trentham Road

A friend of mine had a strange experience whilst driving along the A5035, close to the site of what was the Hem Heath colliery. She was driving towards Trentham at around 8 p.m. in the evening on her way to work, by her own admission at a little over the speed limit. Reaching the top of a hump in the road she was forced to brake sharply as two young men ran across the road and disappeared as they reached the other side.

Shocked, my friend continued her journey at a much more cautious speed and just down the road she saw in front of her the same two young men, this time walking slowly across the road. Along with the fact that the men had bizarrely disappeared from view the first time and the impossible distance they will have had to travel by foot to catch up with her, what was most chilling about this case is that if my friend had not been driving slowly after the first sighting she would have hit the young men and caused a very serious accident.

The A50

If reports are to be believed, the nearby A50 also has a number of ghosts of its own. The A50 is often used as the setting for a 'phantom hitchhiker' tale where a man is picked up on the way from Nottingham to Stoke. He alights a little way down at a petrol station and asks the driver to telephone his wife. Predictably, the wife is aghast and tells the driver that her husband died a year ago that very night. This type of tale is heard across the country in very similar form, and so may well be just an urban myth. However, I also have accounts on record of sightings of figures standing by the side of the road that disappear when they are passed.

Road ghosts are a strange phenomenon, not in the least because the reports range from urban myths through to genuine first-hand experiences with what seem to be ghostly apparitions. Whilst the urban myths may be explained by the fact that roads are naturally isolated and sometimes scary places, and so the perfect setting for an unnerving or gory story, the reports of apparitions have proved a little more difficult to explain away.

As the study that found the M6 to be the most haunted road suggests, there seem to be certain areas where this sort of activity is focussed. It is difficult to say if this is really the case with Stoke, as the stories here relate in the main to two of the major arteries in and out of the city, and so with more people travelling these routes it is likely that more experiences will be reported. A further report that comes from the A34, a well-used route up to Cheshire and Manchester, where two people driving towards Stoke saw the same white-haired man within an improbably short space of time and long distance apart, seems to reinforce this theory. That said, it seems the relatively minor Trentham to Longton road has a tendency to provide occurrences and reports that would not be expected by statistical chance.

A common rational theory as to why people experience road ghosts concerns the fact that most of us will slip into something of a trance when driving long distances. Our peripheral vision and general awareness suffer as a result and this can cause people to think they have seen a figure or other ghostly shape. However, this is not sufficient to explain incidents where the motorist has appeared to hit someone and continued to believe so until they can find no trace of the victim. In a similar way to how psychic mediums claim to alter their brain patterns and 'tune in' to the spirit world, some believe that the trance-like state mentioned above can actually help us to reach a similar plane of consciousness and so make us more likely to witness a ghost. Although this is a rather vague explanation there may be some truth in it, especially where repeat or multiple-witness experiences suggest that there is something present in the environment causing the experiences, and that they are not all in the mind.

KEELE

There are a number of remarkable things to write about the village of Keele and nearby Keele Hall. Not only did the military order, regarded by some as the precursor to the Freemasons, have a base here, legend has it that one of history's

Keele Hall. The hall is said to be haunted by the spirit of a Victorian maid. (Peter Greatbach)

most notorious occultists visited the area and regarded it as having sacred power. On top of this is the range of curious experiences a number of people have had in the imposing hall.

The Templars

A good place to start is the Knights Templar, who many people will have heard of through the popular book *The Da Vinci Code*. Although the interpretation of the Templars' influence offered by Dan Brown is controversial to say the least, the order does have a rather chequered history and they are consistently linked to modern-day groups such as the Freemasons. Indeed, since the 1700s some Masonic groups have claimed a number of their mystical rites to be directly influenced by those of the Templars.

The history of the Poor Fellow-Soldiers of Christ and of the Temple of Solomon, to give the order its full title, dates back to the crusades of the twelfth century. These religious military campaigns were concerned largely with recapturing the Holy Land from Islamic rule, and the success of the first crusade allowed a new wave of pilgrims to make the journey from Europe to places such as Jerusalem. However, travelling to and around the Holy Land was highly dangerous and so a number of Christian military orders formed to help protect travellers. One of the most successful of these was the Knights Templar, which was officially recognised by the Roman Catholic Church and at the peak of its power boasted tremendous wealth and property throughout Europe and the Holy Lands.

Unfortunately, by the start of the fourteenth century their vast wealth and political power appeared to become their undoing, and as the order fell out of favour, rumours spread about strange ceremonial practices and initiation rites. In 1307 Pope Clement did little to stop the arrest, torture and execution of many Templars in France, and under intense pressure he officially disbanded the order in 1312.

Since then, the mystical reputation of the Templars has grown, with a number of later occult and esoteric groups claiming their rituals are taken directly from those of the order. No one has really managed to completely untangle the mystery behind the demise of the order and its subsequent influence on these groups, but it seems certain that there is as much invented nonsense as there is truth.

What we do know for sure is that around 1168 King Henry II gave 'the vill of Keele and its appurtenances' to the Templar, who initially leased the land before establishing a preceptory here some time in the thirteenth century. A preceptory was an important administrative centre in the Templars' system, as civilians leaving on crusades or pilgrimages could leave their money here safe in the knowledge that they would be able to collect it should they be lucky enough to return. The land would have been farmed, and new recruits would have been trained in their allotted job. If the Templars did indeed practice some dark or forbidden religion, then it is probable that these activities – including, it is said, pederasty and the worshipping of a disembodied head – would have been practiced in preceptories such as that at Keele.

Keele Hall

In 1580 the Sneyd family built a grand Tudor house here as a symbol of their wealth and power. After numerous alterations, the house was rebuilt in 1851 in the fashionable neo-Jacobean style by architect Anthony Salvin. Although a successful local family with interests in coal and iron, the Sneyds gave up Keele Hall in the twentieth century, with the exiled Grand Duke Michael of Russia living here between 1901 and 1910. In 1948 the newly-formed university purchased the hall and grounds.

Keele has a strong reputation for hauntings. In the days before the sprawl of the modern university campus, the hall was used both for lectures and seminars and also as accommodation for some of the academic staff. It is known that several people from this time had reported encountering the ghost of a Victorian-era maid on the top floor, which was latterly home to the English department. More recently, what appears to be a time-slip occurred during an event at the hall; university employee Chris Wain explains further:

In about 1999 I was rung up by an elderly lady who had recently attended a lunchtime event at the hall. She seemed quite sincere and described how when the time came to leave she and her husband had been walking to the front door where there are some extremely steep steps. When she got past the Great Hall into the Screens Passage, at the end of which is the front door, the first thing that happened was she caught sight from the corner of her eye of a servant girl in Victorian costume walking along and disappearing into the panelling at the other end of the passage, away from the front door. There are in fact doors in the panelling, so this might have meant no more than that she caught sight of one of the staff using a real door. The next thing that happened was she felt that everything was different from what it had been in some indefinable way. There is a little window to the left of the front door, which looks down onto the courtyard. She described herself as looking out through that, and the courtyard looked quite different from the one she had come through before lunch, though she was unable to describe in what way. She became convinced that she had been transported, not into the past of the present house but into the previous Elizabethan one, which was knocked down for rebuilding in the 1850s. After a moment the vision faded, she came back from the little window, and called out to her husband that they should not try to tackle the steep flight of steps on their own. A few days later, being unable to get these events out of her mind, she decided to report her experience to the university, and was put on to me, as

Lindsey block, Keele; the scene of several ghostly encounters.

the person responsible for taking visitors round the historic hall. She interpreted what happened as a paranormal warning that these steps were too steep for them to manage on their own. I judged (so far as one can from a telephone conversation) that she was quite sincere, though what psychological explanations there may be for her experience I will not venture to suggest.

As Chris remarks, we can only really speculate on what happened here. The theory of a time-slip, where time suddenly fails to work properly and transports us momentarily into a bygone or future era, seems to fit, although of course we have no way of proving this. All the same, having been party to a wide range of paranormal reports it is the like of this that I find the most persuasive. The lady evidently had nothing to gain by telling such a story and had not gone to the press with it. It had no lavish or fantastical detail to suggest at fabrication; it is simply a very strange occurrence that, given the long and interesting history of the Keele area, does not seem out of place.

More curious stories have been cropping up of late in the e-newsletter distributed by John Easom at the university alumni office. One student at Keele in the late 1980s and early 1990s has described several strange experiences:

In 1988 in Lindsey J Block I witnessed a white-cloaked apparition hovering in the middle of my room late one night. It evaporated into my light bulb which made a 'ping' sound at the moment the apparition vanished. On another occasion in J Block, a friend had a rusty grenade in his room. The first time I picked it up 'a ghost walked across my grave' and I dropped it to the floor much to the surprise of those around. A year later, I had a similar reaction to a room: I visited some friends in Barnes. When I entered one of the bedrooms it felt instantly very cold, and it wasn't long before I was physically shaking. The room definitely was giving off an aura of evil and I had to return to the living room. I was told by the then occupants that a murder had happened in that flat the previous year!

Stranger still is Dave Gambling's experience from 1982:

I was walking with a couple of mates after midnight around the old music block and we thought we saw something strange happening in one of the rooms. There was some low lighting on, and we looked in this window, and there seemed to be something strange, almost like a deformed body on the table, with people around it. I swear we did see something odd and it wasn't a hallucination.

Of course, it is easy to be sceptical about the tales from people's student days, given the supposed Bacchanalian lifestyle they are meant to lead. However, what makes Dave Gambling's story persuasive is that a group of people seem to have witnessed the same macabre scene. Were they all hallucinating? Playing a prank? Or did they witness some form of temporary echo from the past?

Crowley at Keele?

Perhaps because of its strong Templar connections, and certainly with the help of the vivid minds of Keele students, a legend has been doing the rounds for many years that the infamous occultist Aleister Crowley visited Keele Hall in the early twentieth century at the behest of the owner Ralph Sneyd. Crowley was both controversial and influential in equal measure, writing a number of books on the occult that many consider to be seminal works. He is perhaps best known nowadays for the tag 'The Wickedest Man in the World', a moniker given to him with some relish by the tabloid press. The story at Keele states that Crowley was attracted by the strong ley lines in the area and focussed on a tunnel in the grounds where he is said to have created a magical creature, known as an egregore, to protect the sanctified spot. Whilst the tunnel itself does exist, evidence of Crowley's visit or any relationship with the Sneyds is much trickier to find. Of course, in his day Crowley was a highly controversial figure who was reviled by many, so the Sneyds would not necessarily have wished to make any connection with Crowley public. However, a private link is still possible, and so a question mark still hangs over the matter.

The tunnel at Keele. Legend has it that Aleister Crowley liked this area so much that he created a magical creature called an egregore to guard it.

Harecastle Hotel, Kidsgrove. The top floor of the hotel is said to be home to a poltergeist.

KIDSGROVE

Growing in the eighteenth century through the success of local mining and iron smelting, Kidsgrove is a small town now mainly home to commuters working in Stoke or up in Manchester. It is home to the lengthy Harecastle canal tunnels, and local legend has it that these are the setting for one of the area's best-known ghost stories – the Kidsgrove Boggart. The nearby Harecastle Hotel is also said to have a haunting of its own, and one of the upper rooms (now unused and sealed off) is apparently plagued by a poltergeist which throws cutlery at staff.

The Boggart

It is the boggart that has attracted the most attention over the years, even leading to modern claims of strange sightings along the stretch of Boathorse Road it is said to haunt. The version of the story told today is something of a mishmash involving folk tradition, local hearsay and a murder.

It is said that in 1839 a murder took place along the Trent & Mersey Canal, the most popular version of the story placing the killing in the Harecastle Tunnel. In the version of the murder as told by historian Philip Leese in his book *The Kidsgrove Boggart and the Black Dog* (by the author's own admission a modern interpretation of the oft-told tale), a young woman arrives by cart in Kidsgrove seeking passage to London, where her husband has gone on ahead to seek work. She eventually finds room on a barge which sets off in the darkness and passes into the tunnel. The next we hear of the young woman is when her headless body is dragged from the water.

Since that time, rumours have spread that if you walk along the lonely lane and past the entrance to the tunnel at night you run the risk of encountering the 'Kitcrew Buggat' as it is known locally. It became a tale to frighten the children and to tell on a stormy night in the local pub after a day down the pit. More recent interpretations actually give the young woman's name as Kit Crewbucket, but of course this is little more than a transparent reworking of the name Kitcrew, as Kidsgrove is known to many locals.

As well as being a great story, what makes this tale interesting are both the links to wider folk traditions and also the number of similar local tales that seem to feed in and out of it.

The boggart (for which there are a number of different names including bogey, bogeyman and the like) is a type of folkloric creature found the length and breadth of the country and across into Ireland. Unfortunately, trying to pin down any typical characteristics of the boggart is difficult as the cultural role this figure has played seems to have changed over time. In some stories, the boggart is a hobgoblin-like mischievous fellow capable of acts we would now attribute to ghosts and poltergeists, whilst in others – such as our tale from Kidsgrove – it is

One of the Harecastle tunnels, Kidsgrove. The older of the two tunnels, where it is said a young woman was murdered, creating the famous Kidsgrove Boggart.

Alongside Boathorse Road, Kidsgrove. It is in this area that the boggart is said to most frequently appear.

an altogether more esoteric proposition, appearing with either a strong link to a certain area of land or as the result of a terrible deed, or sometimes a mixture of both. The story of the Kidsgrove Boggart also has similarities to tales of black dogs (or barguests as they are also known, which of course has strong similarities to the word boggart) as these are often described as being an entity left behind by death and are shape-shifters that often spell impending doom for those unlucky enough to see them. So, we have a strong folklore tradition that seems to have informed the Kidsgrove story.

Philip Leese points out that, in such an industrial area as North Staffordshire life expectancy was short and death, especially for those men working the mines and iron foundries, would often have been brutal. It is understandable therefore that folk were superstitious, and the boggart often served the purpose of being a harbinger of an impending accident or disaster. Kidsgrove people certainly talked of a local boggart well before the murder in the Harecastle tunnel took place; Leese cites the journal of local preacher Hugh Bourne, who writes of the 'Kidcrew Buggat' in an entry from 1816. He describes a creature that stops at the houses of those soon to have an accident and makes fearsome noises. Bourne then, rather confusingly, describes the 'buggat' as being invisible yet also like a half-dressed man running after what appears to be a white dog.

The evidence so far points to a case of a strong folkloric motif finding an ideal real-life occurrence, one that has strong links to the creation of boggarts in other parts of the country, and the two being strongly connected by word of mouth. There are also a number of more modern accounts that may link to the boggart stories, and although these seem to centre largely on a 'black-dog-as-harbinger-of-doom' characteristic rather than any clear links to death or murder it might well be that this sort of sighting was what began the legend in the first place.

We can also look to the parallels with the White Rabbit of Etruria story, detailed in the Hanley section of this book. The Etruria and Kidsgrove stories have very similar patterns, and may well be simply a way for folk to process, accept and remember disturbing happenings. However, this doesn't help us to explain the catalogue of more modern alleged sightings or the strange accounts that come from Clough Hall, just yards from the Harecastle Tunnel in Kidsgrove. Legend has it that a white rabbit has been seen occasionally in this area, although there seems to be no clear link to a death as in the other cases.

A friend of mine called Martin Rogerson lives in the area and often walks his dog along what is know as Carriage Drive, once part of the grand Clough Hall estate. On several occasions I have chatted to Martin about Carriage Drive and he has related tales of how he and his son have experienced uncanny and very pronounced feelings of terror at certain spots, and that a number of other local people have felt the same. What could be the cause of this? If we are looking for a modern-day foul deed to tie all this into, then we have the perfect candidate in

Clough Hall gates, Kidsgrove. The track here leads down to what is known as Carriage Drive, which is said to be haunted.

poor Lesley Whittle. The heir to a small fortune made in the transport business, Lesley was kidnapped in 1975 by Dennis Neilsen, the self-styled 'Black Panther', and died in a drainage shaft in Bath Pool Park, through which Carriage Drive passes. Although there are no clear legends linking the two, we might tentatively suggest that the folk mechanism that may have caused the tales of the Kidsgrove Boggart and the Etruria White Rabbit may also be at play here, subconsciously at work on those who know of the murder and spend time in the area.

A Strange Encounter

In the 1980s a young family were living in the Rookery area of Kidsgrove. It was late one night when Mary woke abruptly with a strange feeling of dread. Looking to the ceiling she saw what she later described to me as a cloudy shape with the face of a middle-aged man floating horizontally and gazing down at her. The apparition laughed in a cruel manner and passed through the wall into the next bedroom, where her two young children were sleeping. Naturally alarmed by this, Mary rushed into the room, but found nothing amiss and the two children fast asleep.

This was the only time something of this kind has happened to Mary before or since, although she remarks that several friends, unaware of her experience, disliked the feeling of the house. One person in particular took one step inside and refused to come any further because he felt it was haunted. At the time the family dog would growl, bark and stare at certain parts of the living room for no apparent reason. The dog did not continue to do this when they moved house some years later.

Alsager Mere

A little to the north of Kidsgrove lies the town of Alsager. The mere that is now bounded in by buildings was once much bigger and had formed an important part of local life since medieval times. It is said that in one leafy corner on the banks of the mere an unhappy man hanged himself. In accordance with the tradition for suicides, when the body was found a stake was driven through the heart and buried not in a churchyard but in a liminal place such as crossroads or a junction. The reason for this was that suicides were believed to create ghosts, and that the use of a stake and burial away from homes was an effective way of deterring any hauntings. However, in this case it does not seem to have worked, as a local legend states that the man's burial place is haunted. Although at first this was said to be an apparition, as with many stories of haunting, the ghost appears to have faded over time and now just the sound of a person weeping can be heard at the spot.

LITTLE MORETON HALL

Little Moreton Hall is one of the best-known Tudor houses in the country. A ramshackle house with bowed beams, uneven floors and traditional long gallery, it is the product of several eras and owners. The Moreton family, from which the house takes its name, are recorded in this area as far back as the thirteenth century, growing in power and wealth to the point when, in 1450, Richard de Moreton was able to commission a great hall which still forms part of the current house. A number of additions were made here and there until the late sixteenth century when the large south wing was added, forming the view of the house that is so famous today. Unfortunately, the Moreton family's fortunes suffered greatly during the Civil War and, although they retained ownership of the hall, their staunch support for the Royalist cause in a largely Parliamentarian area left them financially ruined. They were forced to let the house out, and by the end of the nineteenth century it was in a terrible state of disrepair. It is fortunate that around that time the popularity of antiquarianism and the nascent tourist trade meant the historical importance of the house was recognised, and Elizabeth Moreton oversaw restoration of the building. It stayed in private hands until 1938, when the National Trust assumed ownership.

There are a number of different stories of hauntings associated with the hall, the most famous being that a grey lady haunts the long gallery. There are also stories that talk of the sound of sobbing heard in the chapel, thought to be that of a child. Significantly, there are contemporary reports of visitors who have had unexplained experiences, many of which seem to focus on the long gallery but vary greatly in type and form.

In 1997 the *Congleton Chronicle* related a very odd story from a young girl who had recently visited the hall. When in the upper porch room off the long gallery, the girl had seen what she said to be a 'greasy' ghost staring at her from cracks in the fireplace. Bizarrely, she described the spectre as having green eyes, thick eyebrows and notably large pores. Whilst it could be argued that grey ladies and their ilk are par for the course when it comes to imaginative folk seeking a good ghost story to tell, the experience of a young girl meeting a greasy man behind a fireplace seems a somewhat less likely subject for a supernatural lie. Furthermore, in 1995 two other young visitors had reported seeing a figure dressed in Tudor clothes in the same area.

Other people speak of a more vague unpleasant feeling in that same upper porch room, whilst there are also first-hand reports of footsteps being heard upstairs in the long gallery when no one has been around. Whilst the long gallery is certainly one of the most attractive parts of the house, considering this is a building of many curious parts, it does seem somewhat odd that so many of the reports focus on this one area. To my mind, the courtyard is as evocative of a classic haunted house as the long gallery, yet there are much fewer reports from this area. Is this simply a case of people following the old grey lady stories, or is there something beyond rumours and folklore at play?

LONGTON

One of the six towns brought together when the city of Stoke-on-Trent was created in 1925, the Domesday Book records a settlement in the area of modern-day Longton. Although there is evidence to suggest a castle or fortified manor house of some description existed here, it was not really until the coming of the industrial revolution that the town began to grow. The coal-mining and pottery industries found a home in the Longton area and a number of ceramic manufacturers are still based in the town, despite a sharp decline in recent decades. In terms of the paranormal, Longton is perhaps best known for the Gladstone Pottery Museum, which has appeared on the popular entertainment show *Most Haunted* and has a strong reputation for strange goings on. Yet there are also a few other noteworthy places around the town with tales to tell.

Longton Hall

Although Longton, as with much of the city, has suffered a deep economic downturn in recent times, it would once have been a much more affluent place. Whilst in its industrial heyday the centre of the town would have been pretty grimy and smoggy, around the edges of the town there were a number of bigger houses owned by the richer members of society. One of the grandest was Longton Hall, the gatehouse to which can still be seen on the Longton to Trentham road. We know that a house was on this site since at least 1608, and was reconstructed in an imposing Georgian style by wealthy industrialist Richard Edensor Heathcote in the nineteenth century. It remained in the ownership of the Heathcote family until 1933, and was demolished in 1939.

The chief ghost story concerning the hall is that of a white lady or girl that is said to appear around the gatehouse. She had been seen a number of times in living memory, and some believe her to be the ghost of a servant girl who fell pregnant at the hall in the eighteenth century. Alternatively, we could link in such sightings with the black dogs and white rabbits that seem to frequent the Kidsgrove area and are discussed elsewhere in the book. Author David Bell describes one of the more vivid sightings of the girl, where an ashen-faced motorist wanders into a pub claiming he has just driven through a girl in white. Such stories of road ghosts stretch far back in time, with many having close links to wider folklore themes and urban myths. However, reports such as the one recorded by David Bell suggest that as well as a body of legends on road ghosts, people genuinely experience hauntings whilst driving. Some experiences can be interactive, with ghosts actually hitching a lift with the witness then disappearing during the journey. Others, like the Longton Hall account, entail motorists who are convinced they have hit someone who has suddenly appeared in front of the vehicle. Possible explanations for these incidents are discussed in more detail in the section on road ghosts, but what makes the Longton Hall story interesting is that we have experiences predating the above report that suggest we are looking at elements of both a classic haunting and modern day road-ghost lore.

Tudor Bingo Hall

The erstwhile Tudor Bingo Hall has a strong reputation for being haunted. Andrew Green, a highly respected author and recorder of the paranormal, writes that a member of staff had fallen from the top balcony and died of a broken neck. It seems he still returns to his old workplace, as in 1971 the caretaker witnessed a fleeting black shadow move across the top balcony. Going to investigate further, he saw a 'middle-aged man in dark clothes gliding around the front row of seats', yet the area was empty when he reached it. The same

The Gladstone Pottery Museum is one of the most haunted locations in the city. (By kind permission of Gladstone Pottery Museum)

figure appeared again a few days later, and this time the caretaker's dog is said to have become highly agitated.

The Gladstone Pottery Museum

The location of the current museum has long been associated with the manufacture of pottery, and during the eighteenth century the Shelley family established a successful business here. The site was sold in 1789 and again in 1818. Over the years it was let out to a number of different tenant potters and several major additions and changes to the buildings were made. The modern name is thought to be after the Victorian Prime Minister W.E. Gladstone, who visited the Potteries in 1863. The factory traded under a number of different owners throughout the nineteenth and early twentieth centuries. It survived both World Wars, but finally succumbed to the changing economic landscape, and in March 1960 the ovens were fired for the last time. A decorating and despatch department continued to be run from the site, but in May 1970 the Gladstone works were closed for good. The site was actually due to be demolished and sold on, but a last-minute reprieve was won by a group of people intent on saving the buildings as an example of the many medium-sized potbanks that once dotted the city. It is now a highly successful and unique working museum and a very valuable part of the city's heritage.

Ghostly footsteps are commonly heard near here. (By kind permission of Gladstone Pottery Museum)

Hauntings at the site are not confined to one particular area, although some sections do seem to produce more reports and experiences than others. One of the oft-told tales is that the sound of coal being shovelled into the old bottle kilns ready for firing can still be heard from time to time. A more chilling story is that of a ghost said to hang from a gibbet on the staircase leading to the restaurant, although there is a strong possibility that this was a myth created by a former member of staff. The museum has a number of employees that give live demonstrations to visitors on various parts of the pottery making process and there are first-hand reports from several of them who have had small but unexplained experiences. One employee witnessed a small padlock swing merrily back and forth with no suggestion of human intervention or sufficient drafts or vibrations to cause the movement.

Two areas disliked by many people are the colour gallery and what is known as the doctor's house, the first floor of which is used as offices. A common type of phenomena experienced in the doctor's house is the sound of footsteps with no logical cause. People have experienced a strong sense of presence in these parts of the museum, and a certain degree of folklore has built up around the belief that the colour gallery is in some way the focus of the hauntings. Footsteps are again reported on the stairs leading up to the gallery, and objects have appeared to move of their own accord. However, whilst these reports cannot

The sound of a working pottery, including the shovelling of coal to fire the kilns, is said to be heard late at night. (By kind permission of Gladstone Pottery Museum)

easily be explained, there is no real evidence to suggest this area is the centre of paranormal phenomena. This may instead be down to the combination of a visit from the television show *Most Haunted*, which spent quite a bit of time in this area, and consequent visits from local paranormal groups carrying on where the programme left off. Regardless of this, I can certainly attest that although the site in general has a very welcoming and warm feel to it, even before the visit of *Most Haunted* the museum had a strong reputation amongst staff for ghostly phenomena.

The colour gallery. Some claim this room to be the focus of hauntings on the site. (By kind permission of Gladstone Pottery Museum)

Meir Hay

When a young couple moved into a semi-detached house in the Meir Hay area of Stoke-on-Trent, they seemed to purchase more than just bricks and mortar. One of the vendor's requests made at the time of purchase was that the new owners did not discard boxed personal property belonging to the previous owner that was currently stored in the loft. The proviso was that the property would be collected by the father of the previous owner at a date to be arranged, and although an unusual request the young couple were prepared to put up with the inconvenience, believing that the items would be collected in the near future.

On the day they moved in the new owners were storing some of their own items in the loft when they observed a note attached to the stored boxes, the note read, 'Please do not dispose of these items as they belonged to my recently deceased daughter. I will make arrangements with you to collect them as soon as possible'.

Moving the items to one side of the loft the couple contemplated the contents of the boxes, but respecting the privacy of the owner they left the items in the loft and continued to settle into their new home.

Weeks passed and no one contacted them to arrange collection of the items. The couple approached their estate agent and enquired about contact details so that they could make arrangements to return the property to the family, but the agent was unable to help. A few days later they discussed their quandary with a neighbour who informed them that the property belonged to a young lady who had committed suicide in the house. The couple were alarmed to hear the grisly history of their new home and pushed the neighbour for more information. The young woman had apparently hanged herself somewhere on the first floor of the property following an argument with her partner.

The couple decided to be patient and left the property in the loft for a further six months before taking the decision to dispose of it. It was after doing this that unusual things started to happen, beginning with strange noises in the loft. These usually occurred during the early hours of the morning and included footsteps, knocks and scratches. At first they thought they had mice or birds in the loft and set traps to try and catch the culprits, but traps were unsuccessful and there was never any evidence of animal activity. The party wall in the loft was intact, so the noise was unlikely to be caused by the neighbours, who in any case were very quiet people and had never previously disturbed the couple.

After suffering many restless nights the couple noticed that the activity in the house was changing. They often heard the sound of someone walking around the ground floor of their house coupled with doors opening and closing. The family dogs began to bark at the same time every morning and on many occasions the couple awoke from their slumbers believing there was an intruder in their house. All attempts to investigate the noises had proved to be futile and no cause was ever found. Wondering if somehow the phenomena in the house are related to the disposal of the young lady's possessions the couple have decided to invite paranormal researchers into their house to investigate this activity further.

MINES

Much of Stoke's past economic success was thanks to the coal mines that once littered the North Staffordshire landscape. The Romans are understood to have dug for coal in the Chesterton area, and by the thirteenth century there were more sophisticated operations at Tunstall, Shelton and Keele.

Of course, Stoke is not unique in its strong association with mining. From the extraction of coal in Newcastle-upon-Tyne to lead mining in Cornwall, much of our country must be riddled with pits and shafts beneath the surface. Working conditions for miners have never been ideal and even today the occupation must rank amongst the most inhospitable. Little wonder, then, that a host of legends and folklore have long been associated with mining communities. In Cornwall, for many years there was a strong belief in a type of pixie known as 'knockers' that would be blamed for strange occurrences and accidents. Small explosions and associated noises, which we now know are most likely to be caused by confined gases, were often said to be the work of these folk as they skulked in the dark recesses of the pits.

Perhaps it was easier for people to explain away such mysterious circumstances, and what must have been fairly regular fatal accidents, to such a supernatural force. It is possible that early reports of the Kidsgrove Boggart may have been caused by such a need. Just over the border in Derbyshire, the Blue John Mine near to the village of Castleton is reputed to be haunted by a spectral dog similar to the one linked with the Kidsgrove Boggart. Whilst these pieces of folklore and local legend may be quite easy to find fault with, there are also first-hand experiences from local mines that are less easy to rationalise. The majority of these concern sightings of people, and often these are people that the witness has known. These may be what are called 'crisis apparitions', where a highly emotional event seems to cause a person to project him or herself in the form of an apparition. This happens within a few days before or after the event. Other reports are linked to past events such as tunnel collapses or explosions.

Chatterley Whitfield

Chatterley Whitfield was once the largest colliery in North Staffordshire. Closed as a commercial concern in 1976, the site is a fantastic example of our industrial heritage. Mining in this area dates back to the thirteenth century and we know that by 1750 coal was being collected from Whitfield twice a day. Development in the nineteenth and early twentieth centuries saw Chatterley Whitfield reach the height of its production, becoming the first colliery to reach a yearly output of 1,000,000 tons of saleable coal. After closure in 1976, it became a museum until 1991. It has since lain empty, although the Friends of Chatterley Whitfield are working hard to raise the money needed to open it as a heritage site once again.

It is said that the colliery had its fair share of 'whistlers'. Whistlers were the noises referred to by miners that were often heard at the pit mouth and were thought to forewarn of impending disaster. Local people referred to the Whitfield sounds as the 'Seven Whispers'. Similarly the sound of a pack of dogs (locally known as Gabriel's Hounds), thought to float in the air above the pit, was also associated with a warning of disaster.

Podmore Colliery

Podmore Colliery in Halmer End was smaller than Chatterley, but in 1918 its Minnie Pit was the site of the worst mining disaster ever to occur in North Staffordshire. As with so many accidents of this sort, the cause was thought to be an explosion of gas and coal dust. In total 155 people lost their lives, mostly through carbon-monoxide poisoning rather than the explosion itself.

The effects of the disaster on the local community were profound, with many families losing their only source of income. Amidst the grief and shock emerged a strange story of two young boys who had been due to work down the Minnie Pit that day. On their usual route to work over Boon Hill the two boys saw a large bear appear from the trees and approach them. Naturally, they were shocked and quickly returned home rather than retrace their steps and face the fearsome creature again. It is said that, despite a thorough search of the area, no trace of the bear could be seen and there were no known escapees from local circuses and the like. The folk of Halmer End took the unusual occurrence to be a sign from higher powers intended to protect the young boys from travelling to their deaths in the disaster.

Strangely, Boon Hill is also the site of a much older legend concerning Hugh de Audley, a powerful local landowner in the twelfth century who owned the Hill as part of his large estate. Whilst out hunting here one day, de Audley happened across a bear, which he decided would be a fine trophy and so rode in for the kill. However, as he neared the animal he saw that she had a small cub still dependent on her, and so he decided to spare her life. This has passed into local legend as an example of de Audley's generous personality, and some have speculated that the bear that scared the young boys away from the Minnie Pit disaster may have been the spirit of the same animal spared by de Audley. It would certainly fit in with folk beliefs about how animal spirits can attach themselves to some events or places, such as the white rabbit of Etruria. However, from a cynical point of view, it could be said that the boys were aware of the legend and had simply decided to use it as an excuse for avoiding work that day.

NEWCASTLE-UNDER-LYME

Although technically, and proudly, a separate entity to the city of Stoke-on-Trent, urban sprawl has meant Newcastle-under-Lyme is now part of the continuous spread of the Potteries Urban Area. Although not recorded in the Domesday Book, Newcastle has been an important settlement for many centuries and it has held a market charter since 1173; the name is thought to derive from a castle built here by the Normans in the twelfth century. The success of various trades, including silk and cotton, were the basis of the town's early economy, with coal mining and iron casting rising to prominence during the industrial revolution. When the city of Stoke-on-Trent was formed in 1910, a lack of links to the pottery industry and staunch public opinion against union with the other towns meant Newcastle remained separate.

Today it is a town with some 70,000 residents and a popular place for shopping and nightlife, especially with the students from nearby Keele University. Two cinemas, one past and one present, are the subject of alleged hauntings. The old

Haydon House Hotel, Newcastle-under-Lyme is thought to be haunted since a neighbouring house was converted into the hotel bar.

Rex and Rio cinema was said to play host to the ghost of a woman who walked into the ladies' toilet and disappeared, whilst the current Vue cinema also has a reputation for the paranormal. Built on the site of market buildings that later became retail premises, people are said to experience oppressive feelings and a sense of presence. Strangely, the customer toilets again seem to be a focus for the activity.

The Old Bull's Head is one of the town's oldest public houses and proudly displays details of its ghost story. In a quiet corner to the side of the bar the wall has been painted with the image of a British redcoat soldier. It is said that the poor chap was accidentally shot, perhaps whilst enjoying the hospitality a little too much, in this corner and that from time to time people still catch a glimpse of him sat there as if no time had passed.

The Comfort Inn, a little way out of town on the A34, is also said to have a ghostly visitor, although rather than an apparition this one seems to be aware of its surroundings. Legend has it that he has warned of potential accidents, such as a petrol spillage beneath the building, and helped to avert disaster.

A Strange House

The Brampton has some of the grandest houses in the area, and in the early 1990s, Gary O'Hara worked as an electrical contractor in converting one of these houses into offices. A number of men were working on the project, and over its course many of them experienced a series of strange and unexplained occurrences.

According to Gary, the house had an eerie feeling to it and few of the workers were keen on spending time alone. If they were last out in the evening and had to wait for a lift they would rather do so outside, even if the wintry conditions meant they would be cold and damp. It was said that objects and fittings seemed to move of their own volition, including a very heavy oak door that sometimes moved in a way most unusual for its weight. Many of the solid walls in the house had curious holes in them, running the length of the building and shaped as if someone had run clean through. In one area, the floorboards above the cellar were bowed upwards, with corresponding holes in each of the floors above to the roof.

But perhaps the most puzzling event happened once everyone had gone home. Every night, the workers would pack away their tools and lock them securely in a shed which had only one door. On one occasion they returned the next morning to find the door still locked, but the tools within scattered around and strange symbols scrawled on the walls. No record of these symbols exists, but Gary remembers that there were pentagrams and similar shapes amongst them, suggesting at some sort of occult theme.

Although these incidents may seem the acts of a prankster intent on perpetuating the myths that may have grown around the house, I have known Gary for a number of years and he is not the sort of person to be easily fooled. He does not speak lightly about his time working at the house, and as far as I am concerned this gives the whole account a ring of truth. Moreover, some of the reported phenomena, such as moving the heavy oak door, would have been almost impossible to fake and it is doubtful that anyone would have the motivation to spend the time and energy on such an act when a simpler ruse would have had much the same effect.

Spring Fields Hotel

The erstwhile Spring Fields Hotel is now a modern pub/restaurant combo on the busy A34 between Trent Vale and Newcastle. According to local author Tom Byrne, this is the site of a farm that once belonged to Trentham Priory and supplied much of its food. Byrne writes that a house that once stood opposite contained reused traces of the older medieval buildings, including the remnants of a large barn, and that the cellars of the current Spring Fields Hotel building are said to be those of the old farm house. A number of former residents have reported a sense of being watched and some have also witnessed the apparition of a monk descending the stairs. This report should perhaps be questioned to some degree, as if the building

Whitmore Hall, Newcastle-under-Lyme, has been home to the same family for 900 years. (T. Setterington)

was indeed haunted by a monk from the farm that once stood on the site it seems strange that this spectre should observe the layout of the current building and not the one of the farmhouse he knew. In any case, Byrne observes that the owner of the house at the time called in the parish priest to pray for the ghost, and since then it has not been seen again.

Haydon House Hotel

The Haydon House Hotel has had a strong reputation for hauntings for a number of years. Once called Temple House, it was built in the late nineteenth century by industrialist William Cowlishaw and stayed in the family until being sold to the father of the current owner. Opened as a hotel in 1980, continued success meant that the premises were extended into neighbouring buildings. Legend has it that one of these buildings, formerly 7 Haydon Street, was haunted by a female former resident and that the paranormal activity has continued since the house was converted into the hotel bar. Curiously, according to local hearsay there are two properties in the adjoining Gladstone Street that are also haunted.

A short way out of Newcastle on the road to Market Drayton lies Whitmore Hall. The hall has been home to the same family for 900 years, with much of the Grade I listed current hall having been built in the seventeenth century. As you may expect of a site that has been inhabited for nearly a millennia, there are a few ghosts to be found. Aside from poltergeist-style activity, the spectre of a stable hand is said to haunt the rare Elizabethan stable block.

SIR OLIVER LODGE

Sir Oliver Lodge was born in Penkhull in 1851. A talented scientist, he is responsible for a number of important discoveries including early work on radio transmissions and the electric-spark ignition system used in cars. Quite rightly, it is for these achievements that he is best remembered and in 1928 he was made a freeman of Stoke-on-Trent. Yet Lodge also applied his fine scientific mind to more esoteric matters, concerning himself from the mid-1880s onwards with experiments into both telepathy and the possibility of life after death. This led to his involvement with the Society for Psychical Research, which had been formed in 1882 by a group of scholars and other educated people in order to investigate the paranormal in a balanced manner. The first learned society of its kind, to this day the work of the SPR is an influence on the activities of paranormal groups and organisations.

One of Lodge's earliest forays into paranormal investigation came whilst he was Professor of Physics and Mathematics at Liverpool University. A man called Michael Guthrie had begun to conduct experiments in the city designed to examine the existence of telepathic ability, and with the help of friend Richard Birchall – at that point Hon. Secretary of the Liverpool Literary and Philosophical Society – he had devised an experiment whereby one person endeavoured to transmit the shape of objects and drawings through to a second blindfolded participant using only the power of their mind. The second person, or receiver, was then to draw what they felt was being transmitted. As neither Guthrie nor Birchall had a scientific background they invited Lodge to oversee the trials and advise on how their procedures may be improved. Lodge recognised the scope for fraud and helped to ensure that strict test conditions were maintained to address the problem, such as using objects that he had bought at random and carefully kept private. It is said that Lodge was initially very sceptical, but even with stricter conditions imposed a notably high success rate continued. In one example using two trialists, a paper with a square on one side and a diagonal cross on the other was used. With both subjects blindfolded, the paper was set up so as one side faced each – one of the trialists drew first a square and then a diagonal cross within it.

Lodge was moved by the results, and wrote of his belief that here was some form of what he termed 'thought-transference' at work, although he was mystified as to what that mechanism may be.

This was just the start of his dealings with the paranormal. He became involved with the subject of mediumship and related claims that the spirits of dead people could be contacted. In 1884 he conducted a series of sittings with the well-known medium Eusapia Paladino, and concluded in November in a report to the *Journal of the Society for Psychical Research* that:

> The result of my experience is to convince me that certain phenomena usually considered abnormal do belong to the order of nature, and as a corollary from this, that these phenomena ought to be investigated and recorded by persons and societies interested in natural knowledge.

Although Paladino was accused of fakery on more than one occasion, Lodge stood by his experiences of her abilities and pointed out that the criticisms bore scant resemblance to the phenomena he had recorded in her presence. He continued to investigate mediumship, including with the American medium Leonora Piper who produced some startling information regarding a deceased uncle.

In 1915, Lodge's son Raymond was killed in action during the First World War. Lodge and his wife Mary were naturally distraught, and Mary decided to explore the possibility that they may be able to use mediumship to contact their son. Without Lodge she visited medium Gladys Leonard, who claimed to have received a message from Raymond describing that in the afterlife he had met a friend of his father's named Myers. This was understood to be Frederick Myers, who had been an inaugural member of the Society for Psychical Research, and this instigated Lodge himself to visit Mrs Leonard, who began to relate further messages.

Whilst it would be easy to assume that this was a simple case of the bereaved Lodge family desperate to contact their lost son, there are a few points that make it more difficult to fully accept this view. For example, during one sitting Mrs Leonard was able to describe in detail a photograph featuring Raymond that she was highly unlikely to have had knowledge of, let alone access to.

Lodge produced a number of books and articles, as well as many letters, discussing his views on the paranormal. His time with the Guthrie trials, as well as moving experiences with many of the leading mediums of the day, led him to defend his point of view to the extent that his reputation as a leading scientist was put at stake. Whilst the debate over whether telepathy is fact or fiction and the apparent skills of psychic mediums are as hotly debated as ever, decades of careful research meant Lodge himself was confident that there was something worthwhile investigating. He was not alone amongst his scientific contemporaries – French

Sir Oliver Lodge. Lodge dedicated much of his time to investigating the paranormal.
(T. Setterington)

physiologist Charles Richet and English chemist William Crookes also held strong beliefs in the existence of paranormal phenomena. What is perhaps most remarkable about Lodge and his peers is that they were willing to risk damaging their lofty reputations in the name of paranormal investigation. Despite us being scarcely closer to answering the important questions behind the paranormal, there are few of today's scientists who would even venture to look into the subject, let alone form an opinion and stand by it.

ROBBIE WILLIAMS

Your first impression may be that Robbie Williams is hardly an obvious subject when talking about ghosts and hauntings in Stoke. Yet he has been very open about his enduring interest in all things paranormal and for Halloween 2008 spent a night at the Leopard Hotel in Burslem with members of his family and a number of youngsters from a local council initiative. This is really only the tip of the iceberg, as Williams has professed an interest in a wide range of topics from UFOs through to the use of Ouija boards.

Journalist Jon Ronson wrote a piece for the *Guardian* outlining his rather bizarre trips out into the Nevada desert with Williams in search of UFOs. Ronson claims that since taking a break from music in 2006, the singer has become deeply involved with studying UFO reports and the possibility of extraterrestrial life, scouring websites and attending conferences. Meanwhile, his interest in other aspects of the paranormal, such as hauntings, tarot cards and Ouija boards stretches back to childhood. According to the singer himself, his mother Jan would read tarot cards for friends and possessed books on a range of strange mysteries and occurrences, and these early experiences seem to have contributed to his spiritual dabblings with friends whilst a teenager. In the past Williams has described visiting Church Lawton Hall near Kidsgrove and using a Ouija board to try and contact the dead. Although this attempt seems to have been unsuccessful, many years later Williams lived for a time in a house in LA once owned by Ringo Starr, where he has claimed to have seen the ghost on an old lady sitting in a chair in the house. The house has had a reputation for strange occurrences since Starr's son Zak reported seeing the ghosts of children playing in the garden.

In the same interview Williams announced that he was keen on starting a career as a psychic and television paranormal investigator, although he more recently admitted to Ronson that his experiences with high-profile psychics such as Derek Acorah and a mysterious figure claiming to be a samurai have made him suspicious of such matters. Of course, this isn't necessarily a bad thing – there is often a considerable gap between the reality of paranormal phenomena and what is portrayed on television. Although Ronson is very careful in his article not to mark Williams out as some sort of cranky recluse with the money and time to indulge strange interests, the media does seem to have leaped on the singer's interest in the paranormal and linked it closely to his well-publicised spells in rehab. This seems a real shame as Williams appears to have a genuine interest in all things paranormal.

SPIRITUALISM IN STOKE

In 1848 two young sisters, Kate and Margaret Fox, began to witness strange knocking sounds in their parents' house in Hydesville, New York. Presuming the origin of these noises to be a discarnate spirit the sisters began to interact with it, asking it questions and appearing to get very clear yes and no answers. They believed that the spirit was that of a peddler called Charles B. Rosma, who claimed he had been murdered in the house several years previously. Public interest in the girls burgeoned, and, in an attempt to quell the excitement, the girls were sent away to live with relatives. Yet the noises followed them, only serving to heighten interest.

In the following two years the Fox sisters came to be regarded as talented mediums capable of communication with the spirit world, and tasted fame throughout the United States. They held regular séances in New York and became a focal point for an emerging religious movement – Spiritualism. The seeds of this movement had begun before the Fox sisters' experiences, with thinkers like Andrew Jackson Davis drawing on the work of philosophers such as Emanuel Swedenborg and Franz Mesmer to theorise on the possibilities of survival after death and communication between the living and spirit world. The notion of being able to talk to the dead proved highly attractive to Victorian society, and the Spiritualist movement spread quickly throughout the US and Europe. Although it has faced a number of exposés and a revealing confession by the Fox sisters in their later years, Spiritualism remains popular today and there are a number of churches in Stoke-on-Trent.

Whilst there have undoubtedly been fraudulent mediums in the history of Spiritualism, it is worth noting that many respected figures have produced positive testimonies. Penkhull-born Sir Oliver Lodge spent a lot of time carefully studying famous mediums of the day. Although he did not go as far as fully accepting the theories behind Spiritualism, he did acknowledge that something genuinely unexplained was afoot and he may well have been interested in the careers of two famous mediums from the Spiritualist church in Longton. A visit to the church as a fourteen-year-old in 1903 was the catalyst for Fanny Higginson's long career as a medium, often working in 'trance', where it is claimed spirits are able to take over the medium's body. Fanny proved a highly popular figure, as was her son Gordon, who became known worldwide for his mediumship. Thanks to his mother, Gordon was involved with Spiritualism from an early age. By twelve he was working as a medium across the country, and later began to work abroad too. A popular figure,

Longton Spritualist Church, where several famous Spiritualist mediums began their careers.

Gordon served for many years as the president of the Spiritualists' National Union. He worked both in this capacity and as a performing medium right up until his death in 1993.

THE STAFFORDSHIRE MOORLANDS

Just a few miles north-east of Stoke city centre, the Staffordshire Moorlands stand in sharp contrast to the smoky industrial heritage of the Potteries. A bleak and weather-beaten landscape that wouldn't be out of place in a Brontë novel, the Moorlands has more than its fair share of strangeness. Black dog sightings and UFO encounters are as common as hauntings here and the Moorlands is known by some as a 'window area', meaning that it seems to attract a greater frequency of paranormal reports than would be expected based on its size and population.

Lud's Church

Lud's Church is a beautiful natural canyon in an area known as the Black Forest. A visit here tends to be an eerie experience, especially given the fact that it is well hidden with little warning on approach, and unsurprisingly a clutch of legends

The Staffordshire Moorlands is a mystical place full of legends.

have grown up around it. Perhaps the most famous of these is the strong link to the medieval romance poem 'Sir Gawain and the Green Knight'. The story begins at Arthur's Camelot on New Year's Day, when a strange green knight enters the hall and proposes a challenge: he would allow any of Arthur's men to strike him once, on the condition that he could return the blow a year and a day later. Sir Gawain accepts, takes a swing and severs the green knight's head. However, to Gawain's shock the knight gets to his feet and before leaving reminds him to keep his part of the bargain. A year passes and Gawain reluctantly sets out on a lengthy journey, eventually arriving at the green chapel. He allows his challenger to strike him, yet to his surprise his life is spared, and the green knight explains that the challenge has been created by Arthur's enemy Morgan le Fey. Mainly due to the dialect of the writing, a number of scholars have identified Lud's Church as the likely location for the Green Knight's chapel.

Of course, green knights, green men and their like are a prominent part of British folklore and it is difficult to say where the association with Lud's Church begins. Along with the Gawain story, it was also reputedly a hideout of Robin Hood, which in turn has strong echoes of the green man myth. Perhaps on the most basic level, places of such natural beauty are bound to be connected with unearthly power and possibly used as a place to worship it. This view is strengthened by claims that the name Lud is derived from Lugh, the Celtic god of the sun, which implies that the chasm has been used for religious ceremonies for thousands of years. Another legend

LUDS CHURCH - GRADBACH

Lud's Church. This atmospheric place is home to a number of myths and legends.

Ilam Hall. A once great house, Ilam is said to have several ghosts. (By kind permission of the James Smith Noel Collection, Louisiana State University in Shreveport)

would have it that the ravine is named after a figure of religious dissent. The Lollards were a group of fifteenth-century religious reformers, whose local leader was Walter de Lud-auk. The local militia discovered the Lollards' secret meetings at Lud's Church, and one day ambushed them. Several were killed, including de Lud-auk's young granddaughter, who is said to still haunt the site to this day.

Ilam

Towards the Derbyshire border lies the village of Ilam, which is said to have been a holy place since Saxon times. The local church dates to at least the twelfth century and lies in the grounds of Ilam Hall, where a phantom carriage is said to thunder past. Thought also to have been seen on the road to Throwley, legend has it that those who get in the way of the carriage are soon to meet their fate. Although it is now a youth hostel, Ilam Hall was built as a lavish country residence on the site of a much earlier house. Commissioned as a military hospital during the First World War, a major portion of the grand old building was demolished in the 1930s with

The village of Cauldon Lowe. The hills hereabouts are said to be inhabited by fairy folk.

the rest converted into a youth hostel. That certainly gives the hall the right haunted house credentials and it is said that a number of hauntings still linger from past eras, including the spirit of a lady in white who likes to wake sleeping hostellers.

Fairies

In the dialect of North Staffordshire, the word 'Lowe' or 'Low' denotes an ancient burial mound, with places such as Warslow, Wardlow and Grindlow peppering the Moorlands and neighbouring areas. The village of Cauldon Lowe is home to one of the most renowned legends associated with these prehistoric chambers. In 1847, Mary Howitt wrote of 'The Fairies of the Cauldon Lowe', describing a gentle race of little people that inhabited a nearby hill. To some extent Howitt based her work on much older legends, although in these fairies, brownies and the like were often a far scarier proposition – capable of switching quickly from kindness to cruelty. Local stories even claim fairies were fond of eating human flesh.

The Mermaid of Morridge

One of the strangest Moorlands legends concerns the Morridge Hills. It is said that a mermaid lives in one of the dark secluded pools in this area, and local author

David Bell has identified several myths explaining her presence. One is that a sailor fell in love with a mermaid while away at sea. He brought her back to the town of Leek and hid her in the pool at Morridge. However, the sailor died within a few years and left her stricken, far from the sea. Another story claims the mermaid is a local witch who was chased into the pool, cursing it as she drowned. To this day, it is said that no bird or animal will drink from the water.

A Phantom Horse and Rider

Reports of a phantom horse and rider surface from time to time in the Three Shires Head area. One account comes from a Japanese family who were holidaying in the region and had stopped for a meal at the New Inn in the village of Flash. Shortly after beginning a walk into the hills, they were strolling alongside the river when all but the father of the family saw what they described as a man wearing a funny hat and cloak riding a horse at speed towards them. They dodged out of the way in plenty of time apart from the father, who, despite the cries from his family, only saw the spectre when it was nearly upon him.

This story is not unusual, and another account from 1995 nearby at Cluelow Cross bears some striking similarities. This time a computer engineer was driving alone when the figure of a man with a long beard and tricorn hat suddenly came thundering on horseback towards the car. Despite bracing for a terrible accident, none came and the spectre disappeared. A number of stories place this ghostly horseman riding down the middle of the road and causing havoc with traffic, whilst the tricorn hat (which would quite understandably seem 'funny' to a Japanese family with little knowledge of historic British dress) is also a regular feature. Another commonly reported aspect is that he is carrying a storm lantern.

Intriguingly, there are legends across Europe that speak of a 'Wild Hunt', where a phantom horseman or men ride out across the countryside accompanied by black dogs. Variously said to be King Arthur, Odin or a host of other ancient mythical gods and figures, considering the strong association that the Moorlands has with black dogs (see below) it seems possible that whatever the reason behind these phantom horsemen, there are strong links to wider folklore traditions. Could it be that the black dog and the horseman are one and the same; two sides of the same ghostly coin? This is a tantalising proposition, but if true it does make it difficult to explain why the horseman appears in such distinctive historical garb which appears to date him to just a few centuries ago.

Black Dogs

There are plenty of recorded black dog legends in the region. Fred Brighton's 1937 book, *The Tale of Ipstones*, for example, describes a sizeable black dog that could not be struck down, and sword blows passed straight through it. Other stories of

It was close to the village of Flash that an unfortunate Japanese family encountered a spectral horseman thundering towards them.

Spectral black dogs have long been reported in these parts.

a black dog focus on the village of Longnor, and some claim this spectre is linked to a kindly man who lived in a hut outside the village and was known locally for helping sick animals. It is curious that such stories seem mainly to be found in rural areas; paranormal experiences and even folklore from within the urban areas of Stoke tend to have different themes, yet push further north, either into Kidsgrove or the Moorlands and the black dog stories start to appear. The big question, of course, is what they could be.

These strange creatures have been recorded in folklore and legend for 700 years or more and many regions of the UK have their own name for the phenomena. In Staffordshire this is padfoot. However, despite being a solid part of our folklore for so long, their purpose and reason for being is at best rather vague. Whilst with sightings of other anomalous animals (such as big cats) there is often the strong possibility that they are living beings, the black dog is an altogether different proposition. The tale mentioned above from Ipstones is a case in point, as it contains a definite supernatural edge. A number of very good books have been written on the subject in the past few decades, many of which point to a strange mix of inherited folklore and genuine paranormal experiences, often witnessed by people with little or no prior knowledge of black dog traditions.

From a psychological point of view, it has been suggested that we human beings are prone to experience similar types of paranormal phenomena in certain circumstances. This possibility crops up in a number of different theories and for a number of different reasons. The famous psychologist Carl Jung put forward the notion of 'archetypes', certain images and experiences that seem to have their basis in some curious shared pool of consciousness. Further to this, it has been suggested that black dog sightings may be a result of our longstanding affinity with dogs. In some cases it may simply be that the witness is prone to experiencing such things, whilst in others it may be down to factors in the local environment that are thought to cause paranormal occurrences, with suggestions including the presence of certain sound frequencies below that of human hearing and electromagnetic radiation caused by geological faults.

The Wandering Jew

Another widely-known legend that is heavily linked to the Moorlands area is that of the Wandering Jew. Although the origins are uncertain and different versions abound, this tale began to spread across Europe in the thirteenth century. A common theme amongst the different variants is that the Jew cruelly refuses Jesus either a drink of water or passage through a gateway as he carries his cross to Calvary. This act condemns the Jew to a life without death, doomed to constantly wander the earth as punishment for his sin. Although he ages, whenever he reaches a hundred he reverts back to thirty, the age he was at the time of the crucifixion. The legend has endured across many European countries, giving inspiration to

Gothic and Romantic authors as well as providing a subject for Nazi propaganda. The most common story linking the Wandering Jew with the Staffordshire Moorlands is based in 1648. A wandering stranger enters the house of an elderly man, asking for a drink. The old man is lame and offers his visitor a drink so long as he fetches it himself. In return for the kindness, the stranger tells the man how he can heal his lameness, so long as he remains a faithful Christian for the rest of his days.

What I find most interesting about the Moorlands is the concentration of such a number of stories in a relatively small geographic area. Of course, the bleak landscape is going to cause some people's imagination to go into overdrive, but if the theories about certain environmental factors influencing paranormal experiences are true, then the 'window area' tag earned by the Moorlands makes perfect sense.

STOKE

Confusingly for those new to the city, the name Stoke refers to a town within the conurbation as well as the city as a whole. Whilst the city is Stoke-on-Trent, the town is named Stoke-upon-Trent. Although Hanley is traditionally seen as the city centre, Stoke was chosen as the name for the new city in 1910 because it was home to the main administrative buildings and also the principal rail station. In old-English, the name Stoke means meeting or holy place, and it is thought that a church has stood in the town since at least AD 670. The current church dates to the 1820s, although, what seems to be a rather hastily built stone arch in the grounds is actually the remains of its much older predecessor. Stoke is home to the ornate King's Hall as well as the city's two hospitals, both of which are subject to some fascinating paranormal activity.

The Glebe Hotel

The Glebe Hotel is sited a little way down from the Church of St Peter Advincula in the town centre. Built around 1900, it sits on Glebe Street. Historically, a glebe is an area of land owned by the Roman Catholic and Anglian churches and given out as a 'living' to rectors and other church staff.

Recent landlords of The Glebe have experienced a number of strange occurrences. I am always wary when researching pubs that claim to be haunted, as there is often nothing better for trade than a quaint old pub with a ghostly visitor or two. Although they have spoken openly to me about what they and their customers have seen, the landlords of the Glebe make no attempt to trade on these stories and so we can breathe a little more easily as to their motives for telling us about their experiences.

The Glebe, Stoke. The former landlords have reported a range of paranormal activity.

One ghost that has been seen by a number of people, including several of the family living upstairs, is that of an old gentleman who appears sat quite snugly in the back corner of the pub. On a number of occasions the landlord has locked up and been surprised to see this spectral chap sat there, and he is sometimes mistaken for a rogue customer who has evaded last orders. Poltergeist activity has also been experienced; disembodied footsteps have been heard as well as the sound of talking well after the doors have been closed for the night, while upstairs things are prone to move of their own volition.

As a former hotel in a prominent spot next to the King's Hall, the Glebe will have seen many people pass through over the years. I understand that at the time of writing the premises are up for sale, and it seems unlikely to remain a public house for much longer. If the new owners decide to renovate the building, then it will be interesting to see if this triggers any paranormal activity as there are plenty of precedents for such things.

The Villas

The enduring image of housing in Stoke-on-Trent is one of terraced rows with the roofs barely visible through the smog, with pithead gear and potbanks looming in the background. Yet the other side to this industrial cityscape are the grand houses built for the middle and upper classes, such as the semi-detached properties in Hartshill. Many of these buildings sprang up during the nineteenth century when the fashion was for imposing Gothic mansions and Italianate villas, in the vein of the recently built Trentham Hall. These styles seem to have an eerie feel about them, suggesting at classic haunted tales.

One such story concerns the cluster of houses on London Road in Stoke town known as The Villas. Constructed to the designs of local architect Charles Lynam in the 1850s, The Villas were intended as middle-class residences, but, as with much of the town, they have now fallen on harder times. The stucco finish to the walls has dropped away in places and the bold colours intended to give a Mediterranean feel are now faded. The decline had already begun by 1973, when some of the houses were split into flats and let out, one of which was occupied by a Polish immigrant called Demetrious Myiciura. He had moved to the UK several decades earlier and eked out a very usual living working in the pottery industry, yet his death was highly unusual and has passed into local legend.

Demetrious' body was found by a police officer, and by the look of the scene he had either been trying to protect himself from vampires or prevent himself from becoming one. The body was surrounded with salt and garlic as well as his own urine and faeces, with the cause of death put down to choking on a clove of garlic he had placed in his mouth. As we know, salt and garlic are said to kill vampires, but the mix of excrement that Demtrious had spread on the window is, according to legend, a way to attract them. Sadly, it seems that the cause of this tale is mental illness rather than anything supernatural, but it has passed into local lore and will no doubt be told for years to come. By way of an interesting, if rather ghoulish aside, it is worth noting that just two years later in Eccleshall, which lies just outside Stafford, a young man had killed himself at a crossroads, ringing a friend beforehand in a panicked state to relate how he was turning into a wolf.

Haunted Hospital

The modern North Staffordshire hospital is built on the site of the old medieval hospital of St Loy. Although little is known of the old building it is thought to have been a leper hospital, where victims of the disease were isolated from the surrounding communities. In 1832 it became the local workhouse, a meagre construction which started life as two buildings but was increased in size in 1842 with the addition of a further three Victorian buildings. Men, women and children were segregated in these buildings to prevent the children being influenced by the bad habits of adults. The latter construction, now known as the Parish Buildings, was in use as a school house and child's dormitory for the next sixty years before becoming part of a bigger hospital complex in 1875. The site continued to develop and grow, but the old Parish Buildings remain at the heart of the hospital to this day – complete with its old kitchen range, communal bath and wash rooms to be

Stoke Hospital Parish Buildings. The main hospital for the city was once known as St Loy's and treated lepers.

The ghostly lady
seen at Stoke
Hospital.
(T. Setterington)

found in the basement of the building, and which have recently been protected from ruin by a series of false walls. The existence of these historical buildings and their hidden artefacts has helped to underpin the ghostly history of the site. Numerous ethereal encounters have occurred on the hospital site over the years, a few of which are recounted here.

In the early 1990s a nurse was taking her break with a colleague during a nightshift. The nurses' sitting room at this time occupied an attic room in the older part of the hospital, and had a large window that overlooked an office complex and a glazed fire door leading to the attic landing and staircase. It was sparsely furnished but offered welcome respite away from the busy ward environment.

On this particular night the two colleagues had been enjoying their break for the best part of their allotted hour when an elderly lady appeared at the room and was clearly seen through the glazed panel of the door. She was small in stature with rounded features; her hair was pure white and scraped back from her face. She was wearing a hospital nightdress and could be seen cupping her hands to her eyes as she peered through the door looking directly at the nurses. At this point one of the nurses recognised the lady as being a patient from her ward, stating that the lady was well known for her wandering and suggesting that they should finish their break immediately in order to see the lady safely back down the attic stairs and return her to the ward. It took seconds to gather up their belongings and get to the door, but when the door was opened the elderly lady was nowhere to be seen. The speed of her movement surprised the nurses as she surely could not have made it down the stairs in such a short time. One of the nurses did a brief search of the attic to check that the elderly visitor had not entered one of the other rooms, but having found no evidence of her the nurses made their descent down the attic stairs.

On reaching ward level, the nurses met a colleague and alerted her to the fact that the wandering elderly lady had been upstairs to the attic. The ward nurse looked confused and shocked by this comment, and replied, 'It couldn't have been her; she died a few moments ago!' Astonished by the response the nurses went to the bedside of the now deceased lady and were aghast to see the same rounded features they had seen peering at them through the attic door.

During a busy nightshift the nurse practitioner was conducting routine visits to her wards. It had been a quiet night when she entered a mixed-sex ward. Greeting the staff she made her usual enquiries as to the kind of night they were having and whether there were any problems that she should be made aware of. The nurses were jovial and reported no problems so the nurse practitioner made her goodbyes and turned to leave the ward. Heading back along the main ward corridor she suddenly became aware of noises coming from the kitchen, which sounded as if someone was making a drink. She could clearly hear the sound of crockery being moved around and a cup being stirred and thought this was quite strange as she had just spoken with all of the staff that were on duty. Suspecting a patient was helping themselves to a night-time beverage, she decided to investigate further, as patients were not permitted to enter the kitchen areas.

Approaching the kitchen she was shocked to find the room in darkness, despite the fact noises were still coming from the kitchen and offered a clear indication that someone was in there. As she stepped over the threshold the noises suddenly stopped and she became aware of how cold her surroundings were. She quickly turned on the light to find that she was totally alone in the kitchen. Scared by the realisation that she was indeed alone she backed out of the kitchen and stood for a second to contemplate what had just happened.

'You okay?' a voice questioned. Turning to see who was talking to her she saw the clinical support worker approach her and ask 'What's wrong?' Before the nurse practitioner could answer the support worker enquired, 'You've heard it too, haven't you?' The nurse practitioner, still bemused by what had happened, questioned her colleague about the noises. 'I have heard someone in the kitchen on four different occasions tonight,' the support worker offered, 'and every time I have gone to investigate there is never anybody in there.'

On one of the older nightingale wards in the North Staffordshire hospital many things have happened that can only be described as paranormal. Over the years nurses working on this ward have been exposed to a plethora of strange occurrences which usually take place in isolation. Reports featuring just one witness are often assumed to be cases of misperception or at worst hallucination, and so it can sometimes be difficult to draw any conclusions from them. However, during one shift an event occurred that was witnessed by all of the nurses on duty that day and is therefore worthy of inclusion.

A patient, who had been on the ward for many weeks, had become increasingly confused and noisy. She was a wearisome patient who kept the nurses on their toes with her constant shouts and demands. As well as having to deal with her, the nursing staff spent much of their time deflecting complaints from the other patients who expressed their concerns at not being able to sleep because of the noise. After several long weeks of this behaviour, the staff suddenly noticed a change in her condition. She was quiet and lethargic, refused food and drink and slept for much of the day. Doctors had been to see her and had commenced treatment to help her rally, but despite this there was no improvement in her condition. Her husband had been called and informed of her rapid deterioration and was asked to come to the ward to sit with her as her demise seemed imminent.

She died that afternoon and the ward was tranquil for the first time in weeks. With last offices performed the portering staff arrived to remove the corpse to the hospital mortuary. The nursing staff had carefully screened off the ward so that the other patients could not see the body being removed, which is customary practice, and once the porters had left the nurses resumed their duties and began to open up the bed curtains that shrouded the subdued patients. It was while this was being done that the nursing staff experienced an unnerving event. All at once the staff became aware of the sound of a patient calling, quietly at first and then louder and louder. The similarities to the way the deceased patient had called for attention were obvious, but it was the exactness of the voice that shocked the nursing staff the most. They stood still, looking to each other for an explanation. Sadly none was forthcoming and to this day the nurses believe they had experienced the lingering energy of their noisy patient.

The spirits of children have been reported many times over the decades, and the sightings and experiences may date back to the hospital's history as a workhouse. Curiously, a large number of accounts of children often include a link to fire and many patients experiencing the 'children' often report the smell of smoke and a feeling of immense heat in the ward area. Countless reports also mention the sound of singing or screaming and all of these events seem to take place within a certain part of the new medical building. Reports of ghostly children have been common in the modern building since around 1994, and both staff and patients have reported ghostly visitations during the night-time hours. Mysteriously completed jigsaw puzzles would often appear on the day-room floor, often having been completed, unnoticed, while members of staff were in there relaxing on their break. Patients in bay one would wake up terrified, saying that 'there is a fire and we need to get the children out … can't you hear them screaming?' and patients would often report sightings of wraithlike children running around their beds.

From a period that probably spanned four decades there have been numerous reports from one of the older nightingale wards of a problem with the crash trolley during times of cardiac arrest. Often when very elderly female patients suffered a cardiac arrest, the staff would find it almost impossible to pull the crash trolley from its storage point in the ward. Nurses have suggested that the trolley was being held by an invisible force, often recounting that, 'it was like someone had hold of the trolley and was refusing to let it go'. On one occasion the trolley refused to succumb and the contents had to be transported to the bedside by hand. The maintenance staff had checked out the trolley on many occasions and had found no faults and could therefore offer no explanation for why the trolley refused to move.

In 1989 a staff nurse reported seeing a 'grey' nurse standing beside the bed of one of her patients. This in itself would not be seen as strange except for the fact that the nurse was dressed in an old-fashioned nursing uniform, with starched apron and hat, a long-skirted, high-necked dress and frilly elbow cuffs. Bemused by what she was seeing the staff nurse ventured towards the bed, but with this the spectre disappeared.

On approaching the bedside the staff nurse found the very elderly patient to be in a state of cardiac arrest and after raising the alarm she started to resuscitate the patient. Her colleagues attempted to bring the emergency equipment to the bedside, but once again the crash trolley would not move. In a panic an enrolled nurse attempted to yank the trolley away from its unknown restraint and briefly caught sight of the same ethereal vision in old-fashioned uniform holding the trolley firmly against the wall. The enrolled nurse, unfazed by what she was seeing, was steadfast in her mission and managed to free the trolley and take it to the patient's bedside. However, despite the best efforts of the crash team, the patient did not survive this cardiac arrest. During debrief the nursing staff discussed their ghostly visitor and when recapping on similar experiences decided that whoever their otherworldly visitor was her objective seemed to be the same – to deny resuscitation to particularly elderly patients.

During 2008 the hospital started major construction work, and since its commencement reports of mysterious encounters have increased tenfold. Many people believe that building and refurbishment work can instigate paranormal activity. It has been speculated that, if the stone tape theory – whereby events and emotions are somehow trapped by buildings – is true, then changing around the layout and structure of a building can release that pent-up energy. Alternatively, others have suggested that any increase in activity is down to resident spirits voicing their disapproval at their surroundings being altered.

At the hospital, many reports arising from times of building work describe similar phenomena regarding shadowy figures and shapes. For example, several staff have described sightings of shadows moving along deserted corridors or passing deftly through solid walls. One such report described a shadow of male proportions, drifting along a corridor ahead of a member of staff and passing straight through the locked double doors that lead to an uninhabited ward.

Other reports have included ghostly voices, doors that open and close on their own, singing, whistling and, most recently, the mystifying disappearance and subsequent reappearance of clinical equipment. A nurse that required an oxygen monitoring probe for a sick patient was dismayed that she had been unable to source the necessary equipment. Worried for the welfare of her patient and having exhausted all efforts to borrow this piece of apparatus from another ward, the nurse was heard to moan about the dreadful lack of resources. Turning her back to the patient momentarily to reach for her charts she was surprised when she turned back to face the patient and found the desired piece of equipment sitting on the patient's bed. In spite of enquiries the nurse was unable to establish where the oxygen probe had come from and to this day believes that she had been aided by a supernatural force.

The Hartshill Institute

The Hartshill Working Men's Institution was opened in 1859. Funded by successful potter Colin Minton Campbell, it was intended to be a place for recreation

Hartshill Institute, Stoke. Now a theatre workshop, it is said to be haunted by a former resident of the neighbouring house.

and learning. The distinctive building is now used as a theatre workshop by the Newcastle Players, and for a number of years there have been strong rumours that part of the building is haunted. It is thought that such tales date back to at least the 1960s, when the incumbent president of the theatre company told of a ghostly figure that passed from the balcony into the cottage next door. Writer and Newcastle Players member Geoff Price discusses the ghost in his book on the history of the Institute, remarking that a number of current Players recall being told about the haunting. He suggests the two most likely people to haunt the building would be either a former owner of the cottage or Colin Minton Campbell himself.

STONE

Although nowadays primarily a commuter town for those who work in Stoke and further afield in Manchester and Birmingham, Stone was once a place of greater importance. Lying a little to the north of the town is Bury Bank, which was an important hillfort held by the kingdom of Mercia during Anglo-Saxon times. Some think it may even have been the capital of the kingdom for a time. So the story goes, the Mercian King Wulfhere killed both his sons for converting to Christianity and

St Michael's, Stone. The body of Thomas Meaykin was buried here – folklore has it that he was still alive when he was interred.

Crown Hotel, Stone. A young boy from the Civil War era is said to haunt a tunnel beneath the hotel.

buried them under a pile of stones, hence the town's name. Having later repented and converted to the faith, Wulfhere is understood to have founded a Christian site as penance. It was here that the Augustinians built a priory in 1135 which survived until Henry VIII's dissolution, and on the site of which was later built the present day St Michael's Church. Very little of the priory remains, aside from a vaulted cellar underneath a nearby house and a tomb marking the position of the chancel in the churchyard. During the industrial revolution the town benefited from the coming of the canals, and became famous for its shoemaking and beer brewing.

Thomas Meaykin

A popular story told about the town is that of one Thomas Meaykin. In the late eighteenth century, this young lad had travelled to Stone from the Moorlands to seek employment. He found a position as a servant to the local apothecary and, so the story goes, soon became a popular figure. However, he made what quite literally proved to be a fatal mistake by falling in love with the daughter of his employer – a girl above his class and beyond hope of marrying. The feelings were reciprocal, but the apothecary was far from keen on his daughter marrying a working-class lad. After a mysteriously short illness, Meaykin died and was hastily buried amidst rumours that his employer had used his skill with potions to do away with him. These rumours began to grow, and it is said that Meaykin's favourite pony began to stray into the churchyard and scrape the earth above the grave. This was the final straw for the townsfolk, who called for an official exhumation. This revealed that the coffin lid was scratched, as if by someone trying desperately to escape, and the body turned on its back. So worried were the people of Stone that Meaykin might return to haunt the town in revenge for his untimely death that the body was taken to his native village of Rushton, where it was buried the wrong way round with feet facing west.

The Crown Hotel

The Crown Hotel is one of the dominant buildings in the high street, and is testament to the town's historic importance as a coaching stop on the route between Chester and London. One popular ghost story attached to the building is that there is a tunnel under the hotel, said to lead over to the church, which is home to the ghost of a young boy dressed in rags who died an untimely death.

Priory House

I have a first-hand report of strange occurrences in the house lying over the old priory vaults, which has quite a reputation for being haunted. A woman living in the house during the 1980s, when it was split into flats, experienced what appears to be poltergeist activity. Loud noises would often be heard in the dining room as

Priory House, Stone, was built upon the cellars of the old priory. Poltergeist activity has been reported here.

if someone was banging on the table, and on several occasions this was heard by more than one person, none of whom were near the table at the time. Tins would sometimes 'fly' off the shelves in the pantry, with the smell of stale cabbage often accompanying this activity, and a strong sense of presence was often reported. Our witness also says that the occupants of the flat downstairs had reported seeing the apparition of a young woman.

Some regard the vaults themselves, which could be accessed from the house, as being the centre of the hauntings. Whilst reports of phenomena such as cold spots and unidentified sounds might be quite easily explained by the reputation of the location, other experiences, such as items turning on and off inexplicably, are more difficult to rationalise. Quite why the site of the old priory should be so haunted is a mystery. Its history was not particularly bloody, so we should perhaps look to the house itself for possible causes. A common mistake when looking into the cause of hauntings is to pin them onto the most likely historical period. In this case there seems little evidence to allow us to make a solid connection between the priory itself and the activity, and it may be that the cause could be events that occurred in the house after the priory's demise, or could perhaps even be down to one or more of the building's occupants at the time the activity was reported.

A little way out of the town centre, but rapidly being enclosed by sprawling new housing estates, is the hamlet of Aston-by-Stone. The principal residence here is Aston Hall, and the building has had a colourful history. It was described in William White's 1851 *Gazetteer and Directory of Staffordshire* as, 'a large moated mansion'.

It has been reported that the hall was once home to a poltergeist, and that a young couple, who had recently moved in, experienced a range of unsettling phenomena. This included a terrible sound from the fireplace in the dining room as if the whole thing was being pulled out of position, yet upon inspection there was not a trace of anything having been moved. Other typical poltergeist noises, such as heavy footsteps and general bumps and bangs, also occurred. The consensus was that the house was 'unquiet', and the couple decided to have the house exorcised.

The area around Stone is home to a number of other strange reports. Several of the lanes and roads leading towards nearby Eccleshall are said to be haunted, variously by cavaliers, a man on a bicycle that disappears when motorists pass him and the spectre of a greyhound linked to a woman who drowned herself nearby. To the other side of Stone lie the villages of Hilderstone and Spot Acre, both of which have been the location of weird reports and legends.

According to local legend, a grand hall standing in Hilderstone is said to be haunted by a poltergeist, whilst Spot Acre, reputed to be named after the Anglo-Saxon nobleman Wulfric Spot who died in the early eleventh century, is said to have its very own boggart. However, there are some big differences between this and the more famous Kidsgrove Boggart story. The Spot Acre Boggart is said to be found near the bridge close to the Spotgate Inn on the road to Hilderstone. Whereas the Kidsgrove Boggart is nowadays closely linked to one incident, this example is said to be a shapeshifting being, more akin to the type found in the Harry Potter books. As the accounts I have of this are relatively recent, it may be that the success of Harry Potter has influenced the telling of this story.

TRENTHAM

It is thought that Trentham has been an important place for nearly two millennia, possibly longer. Early records write of Werburgh, daughter of the Anglo-Saxon king Wulfhere, establishing a priory at a place called Trickingham in around AD 680. Although there is some debate over the location of modern-day Trickingham, many historians believe what we now call Trentham to be the likeliest place. In any case, investigations beneath the Norman foundations of the current Trentham parish church have revealed two sets of much earlier stones, with one set believed to be Saxon in origin and dating from around AD 900.

Trentham Mausoleum was once the burial place of the Earls of Sutherland, but the bodies were removed and buried in the neighbouring cemetery in 1907. (T. Setterington)

Trentham Hall and Gardens

The Domesday Book records Trentham as an important place locally, and there was an Augustinian convent based here until around 1536, when Henry VIII's dissolution of the monasteries meant the location passed back into the hands of the crown. It was sold four years later to one James Leveson. His family rose in power and wealth and in 1634 had a new house built. This was quickly superseded in 1690 by another grander residence which can be seen in Robert Plot's *History of Staffordshire*. By this point the Levesons had by marriage become the Leveson-Gowers.

In 1834 George Granville Leveson-Gower invited Charles Barry, soon to become the architect of the new Houses of Parliament, to design a house befitting the family's lofty status. Barry certainly met the challenge and over the next fourteen years he had built an expansive Italianate residence considered to be amongst the best in the country. However, by the early 1900s, industrialisation, with its smoggy air and pollution of the River Trent, meant the family spent little time at Trentham, and in 1911 the estate was first put up for sale. When

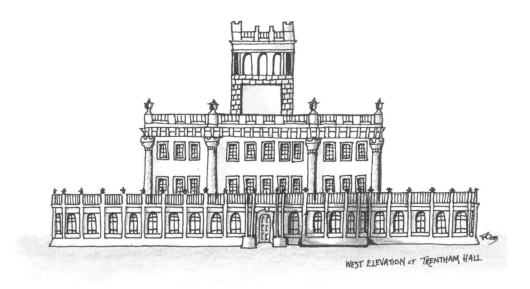

West Elevation of Trentham Hall

Trentham Hall was once regarded as one of the finest houses in England. (T. Setterington)

The remains of the once great house. (T. Setterington)

no buyer was forthcoming it was offered to the local authority. Sadly, the offer was declined and much of the house was demolished, leaving just a handful of outbuildings and a rear portion of the main block. Since then the estate has had a chequered history, but happily a major refurbishment project started several years ago is proving a success.

With such a history, it is unsurprising that there are a number of haunted tales originating from Trentham. The principal story centres around a grey lady, who, legend has it, haunts the Italian garden area of the estate. Although this area was designed alongside the last house by Charles Barry, it will have had earlier uses and is fairly close to the church. Of course, any attempt to put a name to such a legend is pretty futile, and we could speculate that anyone from Werbugh through to the later Leveson-Gower women or servants could be the cause.

However, the prevalence of grey lady stories throughout the UK makes it an interesting point of discussion. Grey lady ghosts are something of a desirable tourism feature for many venerable old houses and castles, and although some examples may be simply an attempt to entice interested visitors, the grey lady stories at Trentham have not been used in any promotional material I am aware of, suggesting that this instance has little to do with wanting to increase tourism. One theory has it that these grey ladies are more along the lines of a boggart creature, and haunt a particular place because of either a terrible occurrence or because the place is sacred. Whether Trentham is the site of Werbugh's Trickingham Priory or not, the area has a long religious history, and some would regard this as the reason why a grey lady is stalking the grounds.

A first-hand story of other strange happenings at Trentham comes from Jon Aldersea. Jon has run a music studio in a part of the hall left standing for the last ten years or so and has had several strange experiences. Despite being the only key holder to his studio, he has opened up in the morning to find things scattered around, despite the area being tidy the night before. He has also had isolated incidents where he has felt a very definite sense of presence behind him, yet turned round to see nothing there. Having spent some time in the studio, I can certainly vouch for it being an atmospheric place. There is a possibility that to some extent this is down to the somewhat dilapidated and suggestive surroundings, so, with the building set for major renovations, it will be interesting to see if similar reports abound when it has a new use.

A Water Ghost?

In the late 1980s, the *News of the World* related the story of a family living in the Trentham area who had been experiencing some very strange paranormal activity. Ten years earlier a teenage girl living next door had been tragically killed in a stream just behind the house, and the family linked this to the mysterious repeated appearance of water in a bedroom of their home. Despite investigations by

Trentham parish church. Legend has it the old church was moved here from Hanchurch by four white mice. (T. Setterington)

plumbers and damp-proofing work, the pools kept returning; a new carpet was ruined and, perhaps most strangely of all, clothes stored in a wardrobe were found wet next to ones that were bone dry.

What makes this story curious is the bizarre nature of the claims – if we are looking at the possibility of fraud, why make up something quite so odd when more conventional claims of a ghostly figure or poltergeist activity would suffice? Looking for a rational cause is also difficult, especially given the fact that the property was investigated by specialists and thoroughly damp-proofed.

Another dimension is added by the long-held belief in a connection between water and the paranormal. In their book *Poltergeists*, Alan Gauld and Tony Cornell write of a haunting in Lancashire in 1968, where large quantities of water allegedly appeared from out of thin air, with family members splashed whilst in bed and a number of ornaments broken by the force of the water. At one point there was such a volume that it had to be swept out of the house. The connections to the Stoke-on-Trent case are obvious, but quite why such things should occur remains a mystery. Gauld and Cornell bring to our attention that much of the activity in the Lancashire case was centred on a teenage girl, and this again provides a parallel with the events in Stoke. The easy association here would be to poltergeist activity, as a popular theory holds that teenagers going through puberty provide some sort of primal energy that powers the phenomena. Perhaps in the Stoke case this has continued in death?

Other thinkers have suggested that water is capable of holding some form of memory, and that it may play a role in the mechanism of hauntings. Out walking with his wife one day, the influential writer T.C. Lethbridge noticed he felt very uncomfortable at a particular spot along a stream. He proposed that water may be able to carry some echo of past events and that this may hold the key to some forms of hauntings. In more recent times this theory has been elaborated on by a number of scientists, including Dr Jacques Benveniste, a world-renowned expert in the field of allergy. He was so certain of a connection that he staked his reputation on the matter.

TUNSTALL

Tunstall is the most northerly of Stoke-on-Trent's six towns and has been known by a number of names during its long history. Historically listed as Turnhill, the public park in the town has the name Tunestal over its gateways. Industrial activity has been linked to the town since 1280 with coal mining and iron ore at its centre, although the town never really grew in size and was still a one street village well into the industrial revolution of the eighteenth century.

In the 1860s, the spire of Dale Hall Church was hit by lightning three times over three consecutive years, leading the local community to believe the church was cursed.

There are several stories about haunted pubs in Tunstall. (T. Setterington)

Tony Hollins describes a ghost report that dates back to the nineteenth century, but suggests that the exact whereabouts of the building is kept anonymous as it is currently a public house. He refers to the building as being situated in 'L….. Road' in Tunstall and recounts a tale told by a local woman who spent a night investigating the property that was a lodging house at the time. Owned by a Mr Fitzgerald, it was said to be haunted by the spirit of a female murder victim and for years this remained the belief of local people. The daring investigator, known as Martha Taylor, admitted having an interest in 'psychic things' and wished to experience the haunting phenomena first-hand. She visited the property late one evening, and met a man she assumed to be the caretaker. However, upon leading her to the allegedly haunted room the figure declared that he was a ghost, and had been frightened to death in the house some ten years previously. Continuing, he asked Martha to 'come close and try and love me a little'. Not comfortable with this bizarre request Martha asked the stranger to explain himself. He said:

One night I ran into a crowd of demons near to my bed, the fright stopped my heart and killed me. Now my hate is so terrible I am here until someone shows me a little pity, sympathy or even love, and then I would be free to leave. I could get away and be happy.

The stranger continued to beg for love and attention. Moved by his story Martha held him to her breast and told the stranger that she loved him. Feeling a cold wind and electric shocks throughout her body the spirit was then gone.

It seems the true story of this lodging house was that Mr Fitzgerald's cousin went mad in the house and killed himself in a fit of morbid terror after a long period of melancholy. Martha Taylor was pleased to have uncovered the truth about the haunting, surprising Mr Fitzgerald with her accuracy, especially when it seems the owner had started the tale about the spirit being that of a murdered female victim in an apparent effort to test the truthfulness of paranormal and psychical investigation.

Although the identity of the public house involved remains a mystery, it may be the very same building as another story that has recently come to light. Video footage of what appears to be a ghost dressed as a cowboy walking through the Ancient Briton pub has been doing the rounds on the internet, and whilst the footage itself may be a little dubious the pub is said to have been haunted for some time. Unfortunately it is now derelict after an arson attack, but it is claimed that it was haunted by the ghost of a small boy.

BIBLIOGRAPHY

BOOKS

Bell, David, *Ghosts and Legends of Staffordshire and the Black Country* (Countryside Books, 1994)

Byrne, Tom, *Tales from the Past* (Ironmarket Press, 1977)

Green, Andrew, *Our Haunted Kingdom* (Fontana, 1974)

Greenslade, M.W. & Pugh, R.B. (editors), 'House of Knights Templar: The preceptory of Keele', *A History of the County of Stafford* Volume 3 (1970)

Hollins, Tony J., *Murder and Other Strange tales of Old Staffordshire* (Debony Publications, 2002)

Jamieson, W.M., *Murders, Myths and Monuments of North Staffordshire* (Westmid Supplies, 1979)

Leese, Philip R., *Kidsgrove Boggart and the Black Dog: A Version of the Story and an Examination of the Written Sources* (Staffordshire Libraries, Arts & Archives, 1989)

Leigh, Fred, *North Staffordshire Myths and Legends*

Pickford, Doug, *Earth Mysteries of the Three Shires* (Churnet Valley Books, 1996)

Raven, Michael, *A Guide to Staffordshire and the Black Country* (2004)

Westwood, Jennifer & Simpson, Jacqueline, *The Lore of the Land* (Penguin, 2006)

WEBSITES

www.film-studios.co.uk
www.ghosts.org.

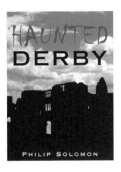